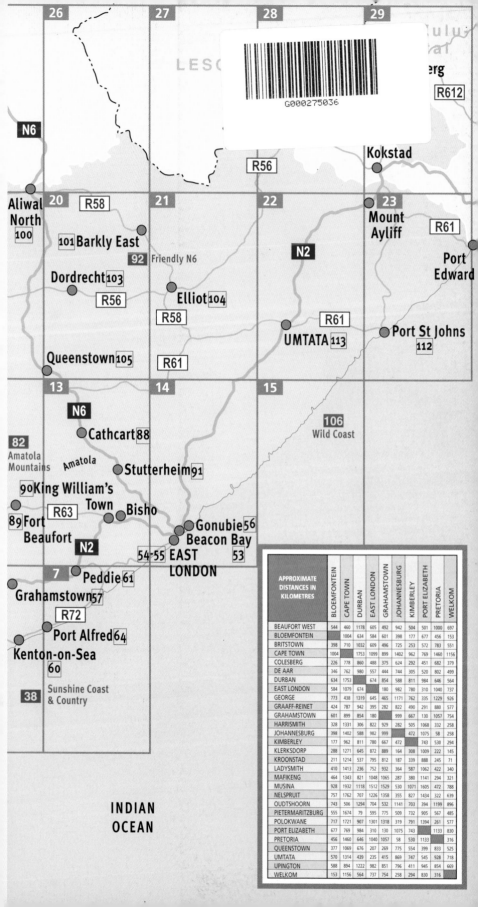

Map labels:

26 · 27 · 28 · 29

LESO... ...erg

R612

N6

R56

Kokstad

20 · R58 · 21 · 22 · 23

Aliwal North 100

101 Barkly East

92 Friendly N6

Dordrecht 103

R56

Elliot 104

R58

Mount Ayliff

N2

R61

R61

UMTATA 113

Port St Johns 112

Port Edward

Queenstown 105

R61

13 · 14 · 15

N6

Cathcart 88

82 Amatola Mountains

Amatola

Stutterheim 91

106 Wild Coast

90 King William's Town

Bisho

89 Fort Beaufort

R63

N2

Gonubie 56

Beacon Bay

54-55 EAST LONDON

53

7 · Peddie 61

Grahamstown 57

R72

Port Alfred 64

Kenton-on-Sea 60

38 Sunshine Coast & Country

INDIAN OCEAN

APPROXIMATE DISTANCES IN KILOMETRES	BLOEMFONTEIN	CAPE TOWN	DURBAN	EAST LONDON	GRAHAMSTOWN	JOHANNESBURG	KIMBERLEY	PORT ELIZABETH	PRETORIA	WELKOM
BEAUFORT WEST	544	460	1178	605	492	942	504	501	1000	697
BLOEMFONTEIN		1004	634	584	601	398	177	677	456	153
BRITSTOWN	398	710	1032	609	496	725	253	572	783	551
CAPE TOWN	1004		1753	1099	899	1402	962	769	1460	1156
COLESBERG	226	778	860	488	375	624	292	451	682	379
DE AAR	346	762	980	557	444	744	305	520	802	499
DURBAN	634	1753		674	854	588	811	984	646	564
EAST LONDON	584	1079	674		180	982	780	310	1040	737
GEORGE	773	438	1319	645	465	1171	762	335	1229	926
GRAAFF-REINET	424	787	942	395	282	822	490	291	880	577
GRAHAMSTOWN	601	899	854	180		999	667	130	1057	754
HARRISMITH	328	1331	306	822	929	282	505	1068	332	258
JOHANNESBURG	398	1402	588	982	999		472	1075	58	258
KIMBERLEY	177	962	811	780	667	472		743	530	294
KLERKSDORP	288	1271	645	872	889	164	308	1009	222	145
KROONSTAD	211	1214	537	795	812	187	339	888	245	71
LADYSMITH	410	1413	236	752	932	364	587	1062	422	340
MAFIKENG	464	1343	821	1048	1065	287	380	1141	294	321
MUSINA	928	1932	1118	1512	1529	530	1071	1605	472	788
NELSPRUIT	757	1762	707	1226	1358	355	827	1434	322	639
OUDTSHOORN	743	506	1294	704	532	1141	703	394	1199	896
PIETERMARITZBURG	555	1674	79	595	775	509	732	905	567	485
POLOKWANE	717	1721	907	1301	1318	319	791	1394	261	577
PORT ELIZABETH	677	769	984	310	130	1075	743		1133	830
PRETORIA	456	1460	646	1040	1057	58	530	1133		316
QUEENSTOWN	377	1069	676	207	269	775	554	399	833	525
UMTATA	570	1314	439	235	415	869	747	545	928	718
UPINGTON	588	894	1222	982	851	796	411	945	854	669
WELKOM	153	1156	564	737	754	258	294	830	316	

This edition published in 2004 by Map Studio

www.mapstudio.co.za
0860 10 50 50

HEAD OFFICE
Cornelis Struik House
80 McKenzie Street
Cape Town
Tel: 021 462 4360

PO Box 1144
Cape Town, 8000

SALES OFFICES
Map Studio Johannesburg
7 Wessel Road, Rivonia
Tel: 011 807 2292

Map Studio Cape Town
Unit 7, M5 Freeway Park
Maitland
Tel: 021 510 4311

Map Studio Durban
Shop 3A, 47 Intersite Avenue
Umgeni Park
Tel: 031 263 1203

ISBN: 1 86809 760 9
10 9 8 7 6 5 4 3 2 1

First edition published in 2001 by
Map Studio.

Printed in Singapore by
Craft Print International Ltd.

Photographic Credits
t = top, c = centre, b = bottom, l = left, r = right
Images of Africa
Colour Library 30t, 31b.
Keith Young cover, 69.
Shaen Adey VI, VII, 30c, 39, 107.
Hein von Horsten III,VIIIt, IX, 31t, 33, 83.
Nigel J Dennis VIIIb.
Mark Skinner 30b.
Walter Knirr IV, 93.
Cover: Donkin Street, Port Elizabeth.
Page III: Baviaanskloof area.
Page IV: Cape Recife.

Map Studio Tourist team
Dénielle Lategan
Edward Hill
Elaine Fick
John Loubser
Lois O'Brien
Mark Hedington
Maryna Beukes
Myrna Collins
Ryan Africa
Simon Lewis
Broderick Kupka (Sales: Johannesburg)
Gina Moniz (Sales: Cape Town / Durban)

Been there, done that?
Please let us know if you find any inter-
esting information on your travels through
the Eastern Cape or notice any changes.
We'll reward the best contributions with
a copy of this guide when we update.

Send your contributions to:
Simon Lewis
Map Studio Tourist
PO Box 1144
Cape Town 8000

or e-mail tourist@mapstudio.co.za

EASTERN CAPE

Introduction Introduction Introd

Although it holds a special place in South African history, the Eastern Cape is a relatively isolated and lonely area. Bypassed by the N1, its very isolation creates the magic around which the region (and its glorious, yet tough, coastline) thrives: solitude, quiet, largely undamaged natural environments, as well as thriving pockets of civilisation (from small towns to larger cities) that are welcoming to visitors and locals alike. The region is also painted with a wide tapestry of cultural influences, from the British 1820 Settlers to the Dutch and German settlers and, of course, the local Xhosa who have lived here for centuries.

FIVE PARKS
Addo Elephant National Park.
Karoo Nature Reserve.
Shamwari Game Reserve.
Mountain Zebra National Park.
Tsitsikamma National Park.

Valley of Desolation near Graaff-Reinet.

FIVE HISTORICAL SIGHTS
Donkin Street, Port Elizabeth.
1820 Settlers Monument, Grahamstown.
Olive Schreiner House, Cradock.
Historical buildings, Graaff-Reinet.
Bushman paintings near Elliot.

FIVE THINGS ANYONE CAN DO
Enjoy the endless unspoiled beaches.
Do a spot of birdwatching.
Absorb the history and culture of the area.
Buy beautiful handcrafted goods from the locals.
See the diverse terrain, from mountains to shoreline.

Colesberg

N1
N10
N9

Northern Cape

R56
N1
Richmond
Middelburg
79

Western Cape
R63
Cradock 77
78 Graaff-Reinet
Mountain Zebra National Park
Karoo Nature Reserve
N1
Pearston 80
R63
N9
Karoo Heartland 68
Somerset East
81
R75
Addo Elephant National Park
Sundays River Valley

Baviaanskloof Wilderness Areas
67 Uitenhage
R62
Joubertina 36
Jeffreys Bay
Kareedouw 37
62-63 PORT ELIZABETH
N2
59
Tsitsikamma National Park
Humansdorp
58
Summerstrand
65
32 Tsitsikamma
St Francis Bay 66

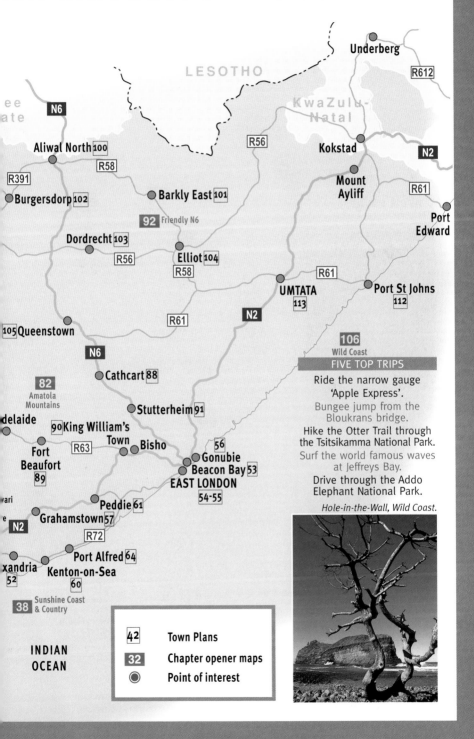

LESOTHO

KwaZulu-Natal

Fee
ate

Underberg

R612

N6

R56

Kokstad

N2

Aliwal North 100

R58

R391

Mount
Ayliff

R61

Burgersdorp 102

Barkly East 101

Port
Edward

92 Friendly N6

Dordrecht 103

R56

Elliot 104

R58

R61

UMTATA
113

Port St Johns
112

105 Queenstown

R61

N2

106
Wild Coast

N6

FIVE TOP TRIPS

82
Amatola
Mountains

Cathcart 88

Ride the narrow gauge
'Apple Express'.

Stutterheim 91

Bungee jump from the
Bloukrans bridge.

delaide

90 King William's
Town

Hike the Otter Trail through
the Tsitsikamma National Park.

Fort
Beaufort
89

R63

Bisho

56

Surf the world famous waves
at Jeffreys Bay.

Gonubie
Beacon Bay 53
EAST LONDON
54-55

Drive through the Addo
Elephant National Park.

ari

Peddie 61

Hole-in-the-Wall, Wild Coast.

e
N2

Grahamstown 57

R72

Port Alfred 64

xandria
52

Kenton-on-Sea
60

38 Sunshine Coast
& Country

**INDIAN
OCEAN**

42	Town Plans
32	Chapter opener maps
◉	Point of interest

Parks and Reserves Parks and

ADDO ELEPHANT NATIONAL PARK

Addo offers the best elephant viewing in the country.

Home to more than 300 elephant.

See elephant, black rhino, buffalo, eland, kudu, red hartebeest, bushbuck, grysbok and duiker.

Hike the Spekboom Trail, which passes through a fenced-off area from which elephants have been excluded.

Addo is home to the world's largest population of the rare flightless dung beetle.

MOUNTAIN ZEBRA NATIONAL PARK

Sanctuary for more than 200 rare Cape Mountain Zebra.

Self-drive game drives during the day.

Many nature and hiking trails.

Many species of bird- and wildlife.

Addo Elephant National Park.

Mountain Zebra National Park.

Point of interest/ park or reserve

Map labels

N1
Oviston
Oviston NR
Colesberg
N10
N9
Northern Cape
N1
R56
Richmond
Middelburg
Western Cape
R63
Graaff-Reinet
Cradoc
Mountain Zebra NP
Valley of Desolation
Karoo NR
Pearston
N9
R63
R75
Somerset East
Addo Elephant National Pa
Sundays River Valley
Baviaanskloof Wilderness Areas
Groendal Wilderness Area
Uitenhage
R62
Whiskey Creek NR
Joubertina
Stinkhout NR
Kabeljous
Keurboom River NR
Kareedouw
Jeffreys NR
PORT ELIZABETH
Formosa NR
N2
Bay
Summerstrand
Tsitsikamma NP
Humansdorp
Huisklip NR
Cape St Francis NR
St Francis Bay

INDIAN OCEAN

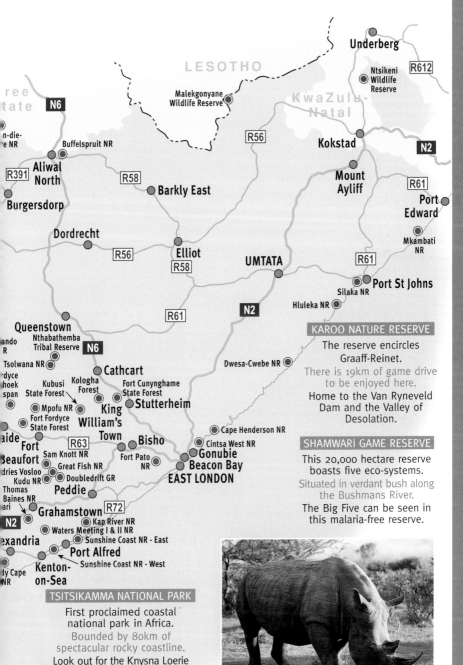

Underberg

Ntsikeni
Wildlife
Reserve

R612

LESOTHO

KwaZulu-
Natal

ree
tate

N6

n-die-
e NR

Buffelspruit NR

Malekgonyane
Wildlife Reserve

R56

Kokstad

N2

R391

**Aliwal
North**

R58

Barkly East

**Mount
Ayliff**

R61

Burgersdorp

**Port
Edward**

Dordrecht

R56

Elliot

R58

UMTATA

R61

Mkambati
NR

Port St Johns

Silaka NR

N2

Hluleka NR

Queenstown

Nthabathemba
Tribal Reserve

N6

Dwesa-Cwebe NR

ando
R

Tsolwana NR

rdyce
hoek
span

Kubusi
State Forest

Kologha
Forest

Cathcart

Fort Cunynghame
State Forest

Mpofu NR

**King
William's
Town**

Stutterheim

Fort Fordyce
State Forest

aide

**Fort
Beaufort**

R63

Sam Knott NR

Great Fish NR

Fort Pato
NR

Bisho

Cape Henderson NR

Cintsa West NR

Gonubie
Beacon Bay
EAST LONDON

dries Vosloo
Kudu NR

Doubledrift GR

Thomas
Baines NR
ari

Peddie

N2

Grahamstown

R72

Kap River NR

Waters Meeting I & II NR

Sunshine Coast NR - East

exandria

Port Alfred

Sunshine Coast NR - West

dy Cape
NR

**Kenton-
on-Sea**

KAROO NATURE RESERVE

The reserve encircles
Graaff-Reinet.
There is 19km of game drive
to be enjoyed here.
Home to the Van Ryneveld
Dam and the Valley of
Desolation.

SHAMWARI GAME RESERVE

This 20,000 hectare reserve
boasts five eco-systems.
Situated in verdant bush along
the Bushmans River.
The Big Five can be seen in
this malaria-free reserve.

TSITSIKAMMA NATIONAL PARK

First proclaimed coastal
national park in Africa.
Bounded by 80km of
spectacular rocky coastline.
Look out for the Knysna Loerie
and the shy Cape Otter.
Home to the Otter Trail.
Indigenous forest and fynbos.

Shamwari Game Reserve.

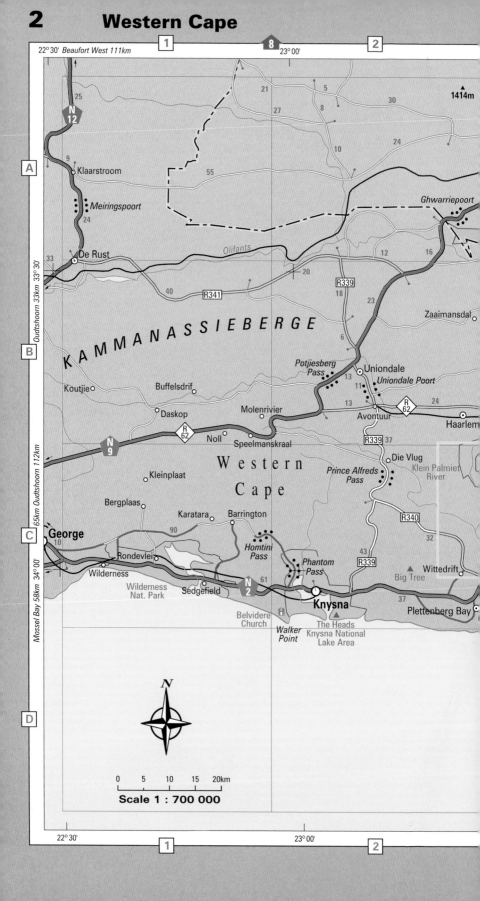

1   **8**   **2**

N12

25

1414m

21

5

30

A

27

8

9 · Klaarstroom

24

10

55

··· *Meiringspoort*
···
24

Ghwarriepoort

Olifants

33

De Rust

12

16

B

Oudtshoorn 33km 33° 30'

20

R339

18

40   **R341**

23

Zaaimansdal

K A M M A N A S S I E B E R G E

6

Potjiesberg Pass

13   Uniondale

Koutjie ·

Buffelsdrif ·

11   *Uniondale Poort*

· Daskop

Molenrivier

13

R62   24

R62
Daskop

Avontuur

Haarlem

N9

Noll

Speelmanskraal

R339   37

W e s t e r n

Kleinplaat ·

· Die Vlug

C a p e

Prince Alfreds Pass

Klein Palmiet River

65km Oudtshoorn 112km

Bergplaas ·

Karatara ·

Barrington

R340

C

George

90

32

10

Rondevlei ·

··· *Homtini Pass*

· *Phantom Pass*

43   **R339**

Wittedrift ·

· Wilderness

Sedgefield

N2 61

Big Tree

Wilderness Nat. Park

Belvidere Church

Knysna

The Heads

37

Plettenberg Bay

Walker Point

Knysna National Lake Area

D

Mossel Bay 58km 34° 00'

N

0   5   10   15   20km

Scale 1 : 700 000

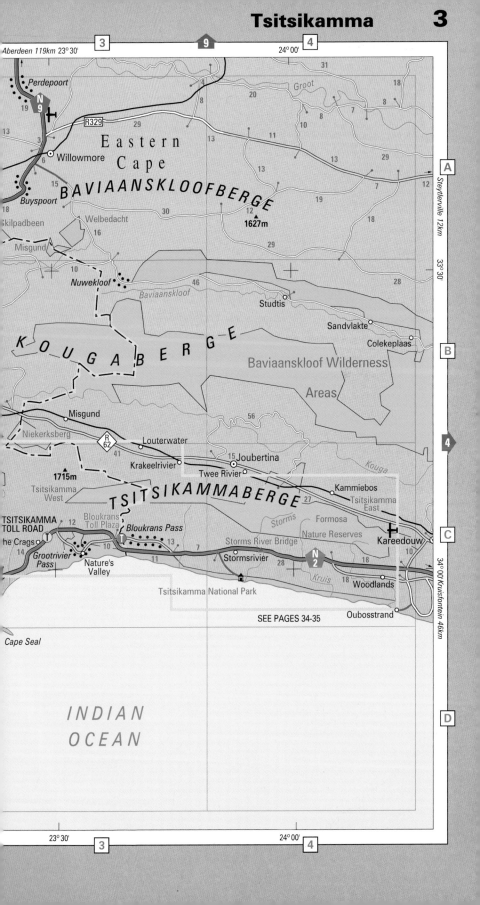

SEE PAGES 34-35

Aberdeen 119km 23° 30'
24° 00'

Perdepoort

19

Willowmore

13

Buyspoort

18

Skilpadbeen

Misgund

10

Nuwekloof

Eastern Cape

BAVIAANSKLOOFBERGE

Welbedacht

16

1627m

29

Baviaanskloof

46

Studtis

K O U G A B E R G E

Baviaanskloof Wilderness

Areas

Misgund

Niekerksberg

R62

Louterwater

41

Krakeelrivier

1715m

Tsitsikamma West

TSITSIKAMMABERGE

Joubertina

Twee Rivier

Kammiebos

Tsitsikamma East

Sandvlakte

Colekeplaas

Kouga

27

Formosa

Nature Reserves

Kareedouw

TSITSIKAMMA TOLL ROAD

he Crags

14

Grootrivier Pass

Nature's Valley

Bloukrans Toll Plaza

Bloukrans Pass

12

10

11

13

7

Storms River Bridge

Stormsrivier

28

Storms

Kruis

N2

18

Woodlands

18

10

Oubosstrand

Tsitsikamma National Park

Cape Seal

I N D I A N
O C E A N

Steytlerville 12km

33° 30'

34° 00' Kruisfontein 46km

A

B

C

D

23° 30'
24° 00'

Klipplaat 34km

Jansenville 52km **2** 25° 00'

A

Willowmore 88km

33° 30'

GROOTRIVIERBERGE

R338

R329

18

17

16

Baroe

R329

15

12

5

6

3

R329

14

10

Noorspoort

Steytlerville

12

5

35

13

11

20

17

9

14

28

16

36

1759m

GROOTWINTERHO

Mierhoopplaat

B

Colekeplaas

101

Cambria

Gamtoos

Kouga Dam

14

Demistkraal

13

112

3

Patensie

Andrieskraal

13

Stinkhoutberg
Nature Reserve

R331

3

Hol

17

R332

Hankey

27

20

Loerie

23

11

8

Van Stadens
Wild Flower Res.

20

7

2

Assegaaibos

15

9

C

34° 00'

Knysna 127km

10

14

7

8

12

9

16

19

8

10

Kareedouw

Churchill Dam

13

11

39

Kabeljous
Nature Reserve

7

Clarkson

N 2

R102

20

9

Kruisfontein

11

8

11

2

7

21

16

10

Jeffreys Bay

15

19

9

Humansdorp

Impofu
Dam

13

R330

15

Aston Bay

Seekoeirivier
Nature Reserve

Paradise Beach

Huisklip
Nature Reserve

13

10

Krombaai

8

Oyster
Bay

Slangrivier

Sea Vista (St. Francis Bay)

Cape St. Francis
Nature Reserve

Cape St. Francis

Cape St. Francis

SEE PAGES 46-47

D

1 24° 30'

2 25° 00'

Greystone

23

21

26

12

6

12

Wolwefontein

6

Kleinpoort

6

5

R 75

16

13

13

23

12

7

17

4

21

10

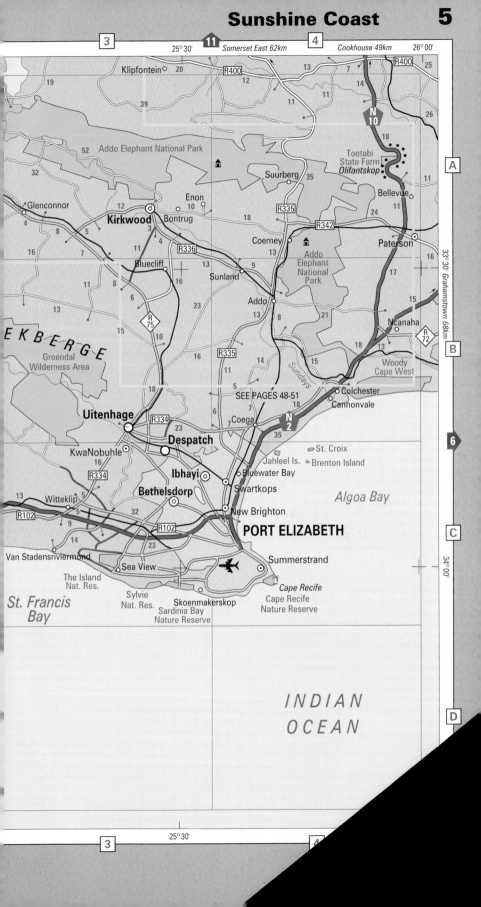

Klipfontein 20 R400 13 7 R400 25
19 12 11 14 N 10
39 11 11 26
52 Addo Elephant National Park 18 Tootabi State Farm *Olifantskop*
32 Suurberg 35 11
Enon Bellevue
Glenconnor 12 10 R335 24 11
Kirkwood Bontrug 18 R342 Paterson
11 Coerney 13 17
Bluecliff R336 13 Addo Elephant National Park 15
Sunland 9 Ncanaha R 72
6 23 Addo 21 13
R 75 13 8 18
15 10 16 R335 14 15 Woody Cape West
E K B E R G E Groendal Wilderness Area 11 5 18
18 SEE PAGES 48-51 Colchester
Uitenhage R334 6 Cannonvale
23 Coega N 2
Despatch 35 St. Croix
KwaNobuhle 16 Jahleel Is. Brenton Island
R334 Bluewater Bay
Ibhayi Swartkops *Algoa Bay*
Bethelsdorp New Brighton
Witteklip 32 **PORT ELIZABETH**
R102 R102
Van Stadensriviermond 23 Summerstrand
14 Sea View *Cape Recife*
The Island Nat. Res. Sylvie Nat. Res. Skoenmakerskop Cape Recife Nature Reserve
St. Francis Bay Sardinia Bay Nature Reserve

INDIAN OCEAN

25° 30' Somerset East 62km Cookhouse 49km 26° 00'
33°30' Grahamstown 68km
34° 00'

1

12

2

26° 00'

Bedford 75 km

26° 30'

Fort Beaufort 61km

25

19

16

Helspoort

R344

24

15

Committees

R400

Riebeek East

R350

12

Ecca

8

21

3

4

14

26

21

24

18

R 67

GRAHAMSTOWN

Fort Selwyn

21

22

24

Old Provost

9

Beggar's Bush

10

A

11

Alicedale

6

5

Kowie

26

R 67

Bellevue

Shamwari Game Res.

610

Thomas Baines Nat. Res.

27

10

13

14

19

7

Waters Meeting II Nat. Res.

13

Langholm

33° 30'

Paterson

21

15

Salem

7

21

16

Nolukhanyo

N 2

3

16

8

Kariega

4

Waters Meeting I Nat. Res.

3

Bathurst

15

Bushmans

18

10

R343

17

15

9

Southwell

15

11

16

10

Amakhala Game Reserve

12

27

11

10

R 72

R 72

B

Congas Kraal Nat. Res.

14

Soucie

Kasouga

Marselle

Sunshine Coast Nat. Res. - West

Boschhoek

11

Boxwood

Alexandria

13

6

10

5

Kariega

Kenton-on-Sea

Kwanonqubela

19

5

Boesmansriviermond

Port Elizabeth 63km

Boknesstrand (Richmond)

5

Kwaaihoek

Woody Cape Nature Reserve

Dias Cross

Cannon Rocks

Woody Cape

Cape Padrone

5

Algoa Bay

Bird Island

SEE PAGES 40-45

C

34° 00'

26° 00'

26° 30'

2

27° 00'

Watch
▲Tower

13

R
72

Chalumna

Xhama

3

Kidd's
Beach

Kidd's
Beach

5

395

15

7

6

Peddie

14

Cross Road

6

6

18

Kayser's Beach

Kayser's
Beach

20

13

**N
2**

8

17

Wooldridge

5

Bell

Chalumna

A

20

5

23

8

19

Hamburg

33° 30'

Kap River

11

22

Wesley

Fallodon

13

Begha Mouth

11

5

22

11

18

14

R
72

5

B

INDIAN
OCEAN

21

10

5

Great Fish Point

16

Kleinemonde

Settlers
⌂Church

Seafield

Nkwenkwezi

15

Sunshine Coast Nat. Res.- East

Port Alfred

33° 30'

C

34° 00'

D

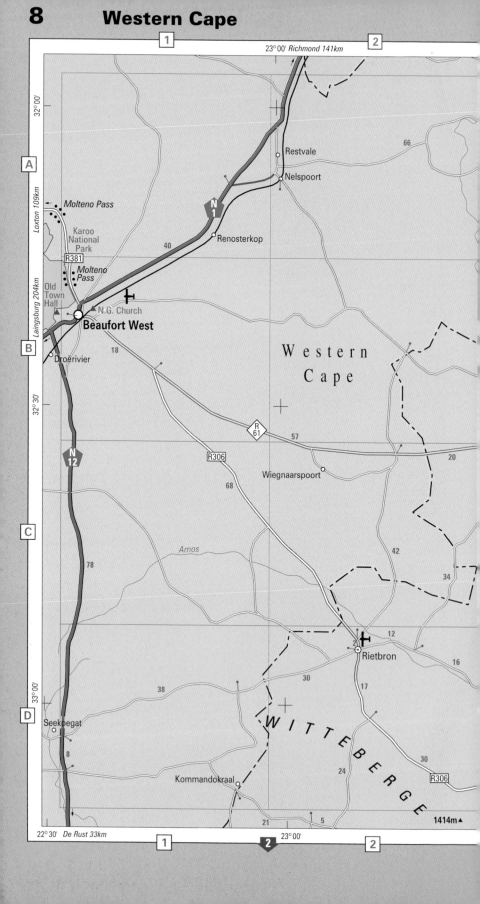

23° 00' Richmond 141km

32° 00'

1

2

A

66

Restvale

Nelspoort

Loxton 109km

Molteno Pass

N
1

Karoo
National
Park

R381

40

Renosterkop

*Molteno
Pass*

Laingsburg 204km

Old
Town
Hall

N.G. Church

Beaufort West

B

Droërivier

18

**W e s t e r n
C a p e**

32° 30'

N
12

R
61

57

R306

20

68

Wiegnaarspoort

C

Amos

42

78

34

12

Rietbron

16

30

17

33° 00'

38

W I T T E B E R G E

D

Seekoegat

8

24

30

R306

Kommandokraal

21

5

1414m▲

22° 30' De Rust 33km

1

2

23° 00'

2

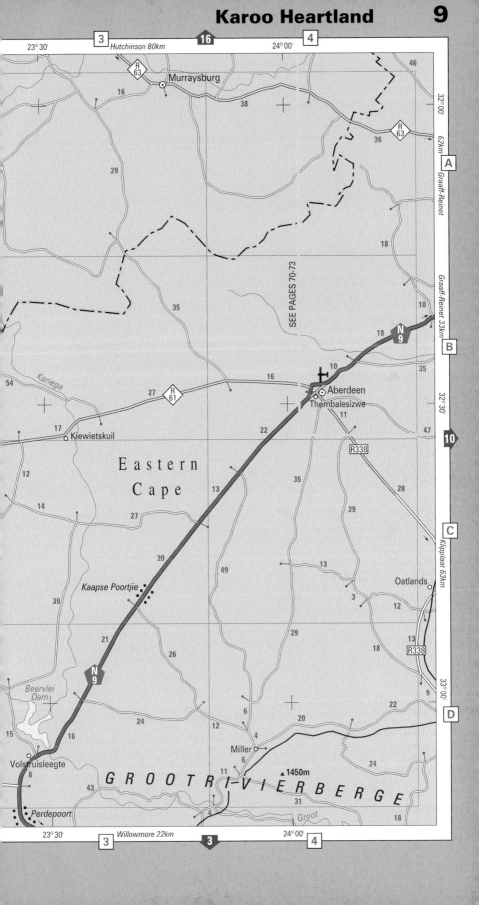

Map labels:

23° 30'
24° 00'

3 Hutchinson 80km 16 4

32° 00'
62km Graaff-Reinet

R63 Murraysburg
16
38
46
R63
36
29
A
18
35
Graaff-Reinet 33km
SEE PAGES 70-73
10
18 N9
B
32° 30'
10
54 Kariega
27 R61 Aberdeen
Thembalesizwe
16
35
17 Kiewietskuil
22
11
47
10
12
E a s t e r n
C a p e
R338
13
35
29
28
14
27
C
20
49
13
Kaapse Poortjie
3 Oatlands
39
12
Klipplaat 63km
21
26
29
18 13
N9
R338
Beervlei Dam
9
6
22 D
15
24
12
20 33° 00'
4
16
Miller
6
24
Volstruisleegte
8
11 ▲1450m
G R O O T R I V I E R B E R G E
43
31
Perdepoort
4 Groot 18

23° 30'
24° 00'

3 Willowmore 22km 3 4

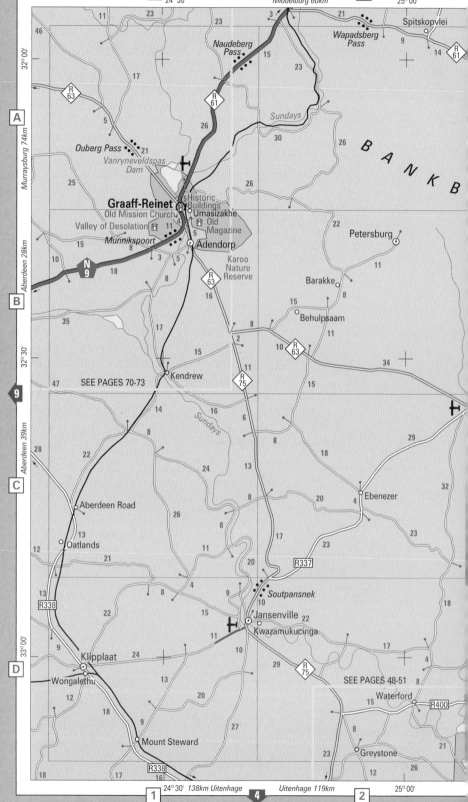

46
11
23
23
21
Spitskopvlei
Wapadsberg
Pass
9
Naudeberg
Pass
15
R
61
14

A

17
23

R
63

26

R
61

Sundays
30
26

B A N K B

5

Ouberg Pass
21
Vanryneveldspas
Dam
26

25
26

22
Petersburg

Graaff-Reinet
Historic
Buildings
Old Mission Church
Umasizakhe
Old
Magazine
Valley of Desolation
11
4
5
Adendorp
11
Barakke
8

15
Behulpsaam

B

8
3
5
Karoo
Nature
Reserve
15
8
11

35

N
9
18
8
R
63
16
2
10
R
63
34

17
15
11
R
75

9

47
Kendrew
14
16
6
15

C

22
8
24
13
18
29

28
Aberdeen Road
26
8
20
4
Ebenezer
32

13
Oatlands
11
17
23
23

12
21
20
R337

13
8
15
Soutpansnek
10
18

R338
22
9
Jansenville
22
Kwazamukucinga

D

9
Klipplaat
24
10
17
4
Wongalethu
13
29
R
75

SEE PAGES 48-51
15
Waterford
R400

12
18
20
27
8

9
23
Greystone
21
Mount Steward
12
26

18
17
R338
16

Middelburg 94km 25° 30' *Hofmeyr 56km* 56km 26° 00'

Baroda

R390

33 21 27 48

24 R61 Post Chalmers N10

Agter Sneeuberg

19 8 6 5 Cradock

A

Mountain Zebra National Park

Old Parsonage 13 Lingelihle

R61

24 Elandsdrif

Lake Arthur

E R G

Olive Schreiner's Grave Halesowen

27 35

2013m 52

R390

Swaershoek Pass

SEE PAGES 74-75 Mortimer

R337 24 12 **B**

Drennan

Swaershoek 31 Daggaboersnek

37 28

R337 14 *Daggaboersnek*

Witmos

32° 30'

Pearston 27 **12**

Khanyiso 34 7

37 25 21 R63

Bruintjieshoogte R63 6 8 Historic Buildings Eastpoort **C**

56 Kwanojoli Bhongweni 22

Somerset East 18 Cookhouse

12 11

18 Golden Valley 20

27 7

Long Hope 11

6 23

16 37 8 Middleton

13 8 20

32 6 14 7 N10 Sheldon

12 11 11 11 **D**

23 5 17

18 26

Darlington Dam 5 11 7 Middlewater 11

20 R335

Klipfontein 16 7

R400 13 R400 25

19 12

25° 30' *70km Paterson 43km* 26° 00'

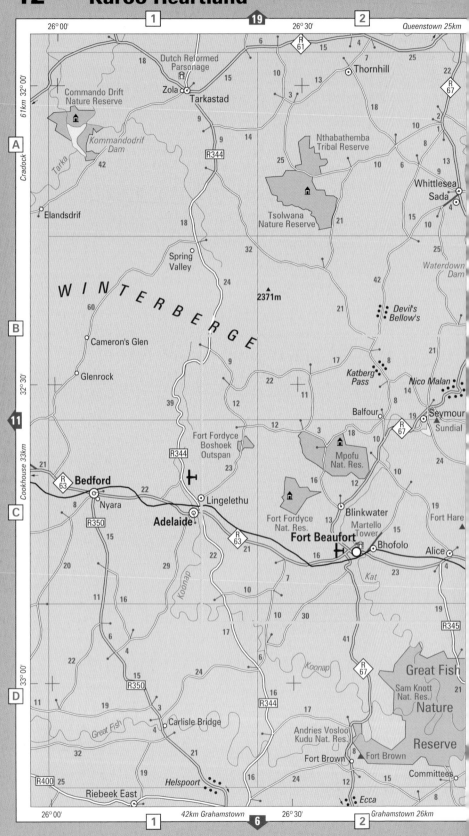

3 · 20 · 4 · 27° 30'

Butterworth 81km

19
22
Ilinge
Bolotwa
8
Qamata
12
Qombolo

23
R61
St. Marks
14
Cofimvaba
19
Hange

15
N6
11
10
17

A

32° 00'

15
Tylden
Ubanzi
Mbulu

14
14
Black Kei
R352
14

20
Waqu
20
Great Kei

28
17
48
R351
39

16
Cathcart
6
Kati-Kati
26
Bolo
21

R67
17
R351
10
14
1820 Settlers Milestones
11
30
14
Bolo

11
20
33
17
R345
21
7
16
R352
18
Mgwali
26

B

32° 30'

8
15
Dohne
14

9
Stutterheim
Mlungisi
10

16
Hogsback
Gudu Dam
Kubisi
R352
Wriggleswade Dam
17
5

21
19
16
Kubisi
11
16
13
Komga 19km

14

16
11
2
15
Amabele
5

Keiskammahoek
Sandile's Grave
R346
10
Kei Road
4
22
N6

Sandile Dam
Red Hill Pass
Rooikrans Dam
14
9
20
3

15
Gaika's Grave
21
KwaMangati
13
11

C

39km East London 32km

Fort Hare
29
Braunschweig
14
R63
17
Bisho

Middledrift
R63
18
24
Bisho
13
10
18
14

19
Dimbasa
Berlin
15
R346

SEE PAGES 84-87
King William's Town
Breidbach
13

Kwa-Pita
38
Ginsberg
Zwelitsha
13
Ndevana
Potsdam

Fort Willshire
41
N2
13
17
R346
16
Eocene Fossil Site
Fort Pato Nat. Res.
25

D

33° 00'

East London 32km

Doubledrift Game Res.
Keiskamma
Sittingbourne
19
Fort Pato Nat. Res.
East London Coast Nature Reserves
20

Breakfast Vlei
12
9
23
R347
19
27
3

Sam Knott Nat. Res.
R345
5
18
Watch Tower
15
R72
Chalumna
Kidd's Beach

17
13
7
14
5
6
Cross Road
Xhama
Kidd's Beach

Peddie
18

27° 00'
27° 30'

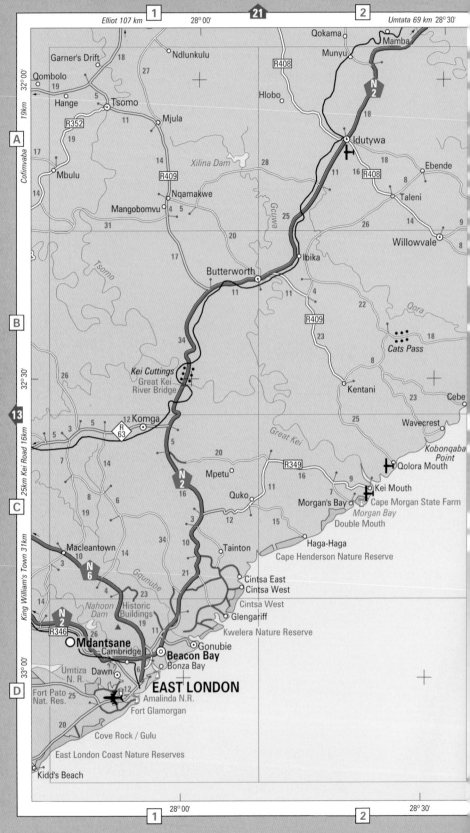

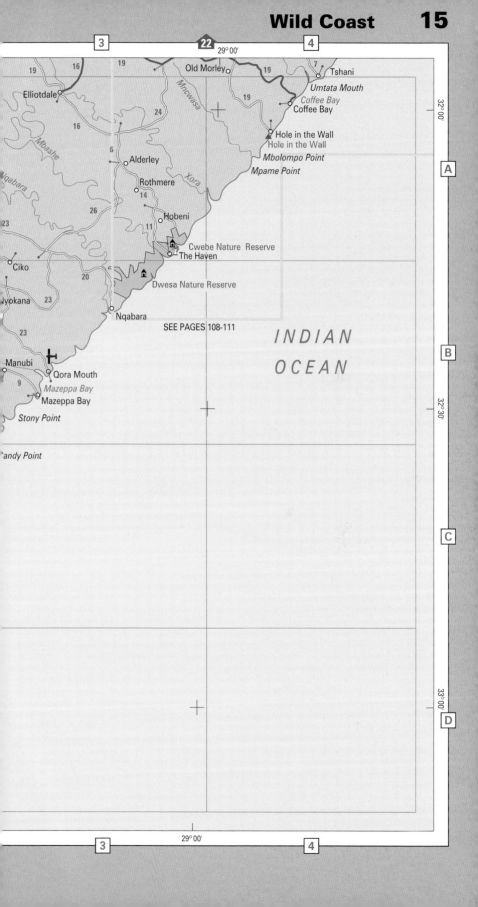

29° 00'

19   16   19   Old Morley   19   7   Tshani

19   *Mntata Mouth*

Mncwasa   19   *Coffee Bay*

Elliotdale   Coffee Bay

24   Hole in the Wall

16   Hole in the Wall

Mbashe   6   Alderley   *Mbolompo Point*

Xora   *Mpame Point*

Nqabara   Rothmere   14

26   Hobeni

23   11

Cwebe Nature Reserve

Ciko   The Haven

20   Dwesa Nature Reserve

Jyokana   23

23   Nqabara   SEE PAGES 108-111

INDIAN

Manubi   *OCEAN*

9   Qora Mouth

Mazeppa Bay

Mazeppa Bay

Stony Point

andy Point

32° 00'   **A**

B   32° 30'

C   33° 00'

D

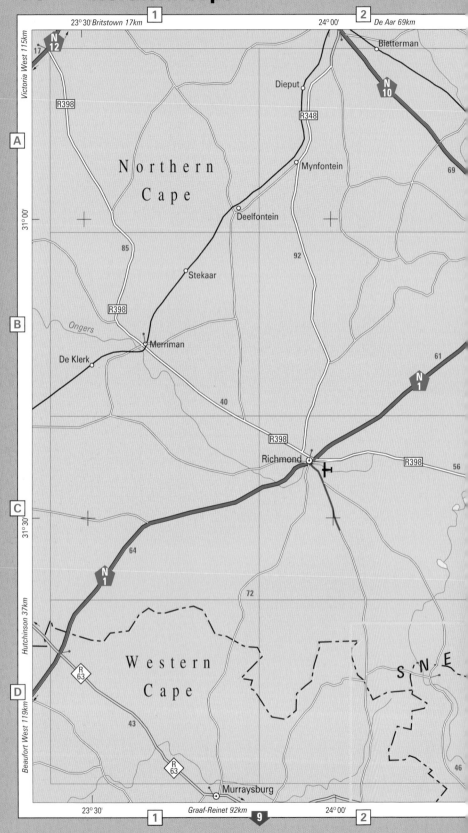

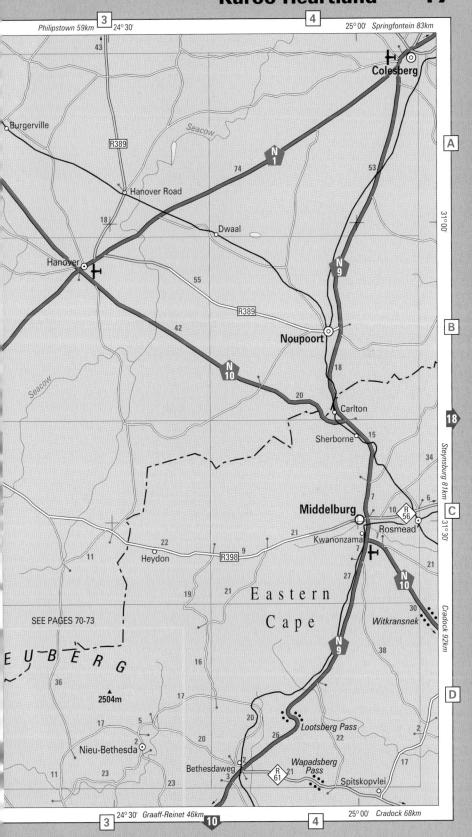

43

Colesberg

Burgerville

R389

Seacow

74

N1

53

A

31° 00'

Hanover Road

Dwaal

18

N9

Hanover

55

R389

42

N10

Noupoort

B

Seacow

20

18

Carlton

Sherborne

15

34

Steynsburg 81km

18

7

Middelburg

10 R56

6

C

31° 30'

21

Kwanonzama

Rosmead

22

R398

9

7

Heydon

11

27

21

N10

19

21

E a s t e r n

30

Witkransnek

Cradock 92km

SEE PAGES 70-73

C a p e

N9

38

E U B E R G

36

16

17

D

▲ 2504m

17

5

20

2

Nieu-Bethesda

20

26

Lootsberg Pass

22

2

11

23

Bethesdaweg

2

R61

Wapadsberg Pass

17

23

3

21

Spitskopvlei

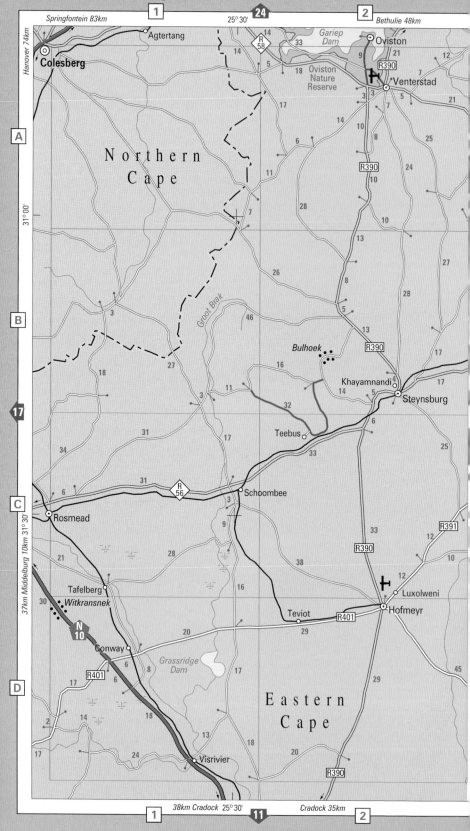

Hanover 74km

Agtertang

58 R 14

Gariep Dam

Oviston

R390 9

12

Colesberg 33

21

Oviston Nature Reserve

18

Venterstad

3 3

7

5

21

A

Northern Cape

14

10

25

6

8

24

R390

31°00'

11

10

10

28

13

8

27

B

Groot Brak

3

46

5

13

R390

18

Bulhoek

16

17

27

Khayamnandi 4 17

3

11

14

Steynsburg

17

31

17

32

Teebus

5

6

34

33

25

31

R 56

3

Schoombee

33

R391

C

Rosmead

9

R390 12

37km Middelburg 10km 31°30'

21

28

38

10

Tafelberg

16

12

Witkransnek

Luxolweni

30

Teviot R401 Hofmeyr

N 10

20

29

Conway

6

Grassridge Dam

45

D

17 R401

17

29

14

18

13

2

24

18

20

Eastern Cape

17

Visrivier

R390

26° 00' 25 26° 30' 4 *Rouxville 34km*

3

R58

Dukathole **Aliwal North**

8 2 4 5 6
Knapdaar 12 10 8 14 16 19

9 7 6 13 10 **A**

16 27 N6 13 31° 00'

R58 17 13 19 23 25

20 13 20 6 23 13 Vineyard

8 5 22

38 *Taalmonument* 13 26 SEE PAGES 94–99 31

Burgersdorp 18 31

Mzamomhle 6 5 Masakhane 8

49 15 9 Jamestown

17 39 Witkop 21 6

29 R391 44 26 13 **B**

15 R56 20 13

9 12 11 13

Stormberg 20 11

23 *Groot Doringhoek* 16 14 26

9 10 **20** *Dorrecht 26km*

▲109m Nomonde 13 R56 18

Molteno 10 5 *Penhoek Pass* 10

6 15 *Syfergat* **S T O R M B E R G**

14 R397 21 **C** 31° 30'

6 14 *Boesmanshoek* 24 R344 52

18 **Sterkstroom** Masakhe 14

B 23 9 16

33 R397 10

A 18 8 R397 **N6**

M R344 16 9 2 17 21

B *Elands* 37 25 42 **D**

R401 22 Bailey

Sunken Garden

6 15 19 **Queenstown**

R61 Bowker's Park *Cathcart 60km*

18 10 **Thornhill** 7 25 **Mlungisi** 6 4

27° 00' · Zastron 83km · 26 · 27° 30'

1 · 2

Aliwal North 48 km

28 · R58

19

White Kei

27

34

8 · Lady Grey

Kwezi-Naledi

13

45

38

10 · Karringmelkspruit

15

10

4

New England

14

17

R392

A

Vineyard

19

21

14

8

5

Nkululeko

24

4

31° 00'

22

Clanville

17

Barkly East

N6

6

13

R396

17

35

16

Clifford

R58

Masakhane

8

14

3

15

Jamestown

17

8

Rossouw

B

6

Queenstown 101km

33

11 · 10

16

12

31

43

Swempoort

10

R392

5

26

11

9

13

Morristown

19

18 · R56

Dordrecht

4

32

R396

13

20

Molteno 46km

8

Sinakho

32

22 · R56

Ida

Xalanga

S T O R M B E R G

Indwe · Mavuya

C

2127m ▲

13

31° 30'

Doringrivierdam

Garryowen

21

R344

52

24

SEE PAGES 94-99

R396

45

31

R392

White Kei

5 · Askeaton

Braunville

19

KuNdonga

Lufuta

16

16

Qoqodala

Lady Frere

24

Bukwana

Ncora Dam

D

19

25

16

Lubisi Dam

Nququ

Aliwal North 163km

Driver's Drift

Xonxa Dam

Southeyville

Sunken Garden

R396

13

16

16

23

Queenstown

8

16

21

Mlungisi

Ezibeleni

8

N6

19

Qamata

12

Ilinge

Cathcart 60km · 27° 00' · 1 · **13** · 2 · 27° 30'

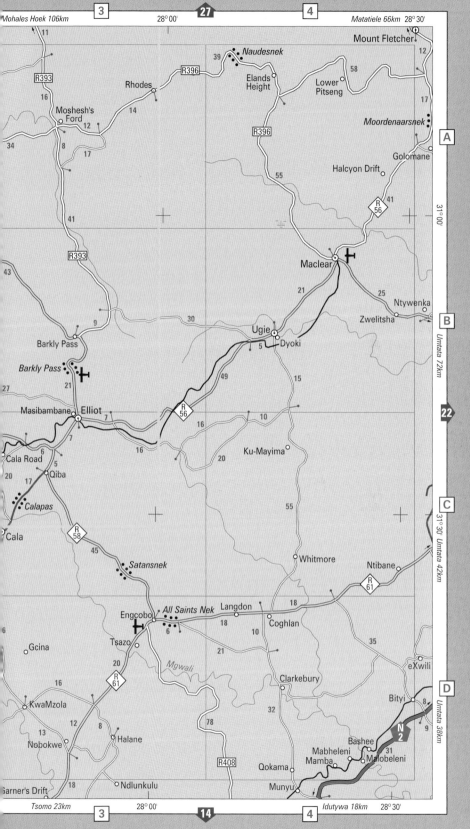

Mount Fletcher

11

12

R393

58

Rhodes

R396

39 Naudesnek

Elands
Height

Lower
Pitseng

17

16

14

Moshesh's
Ford

12

Moordenaarsnek

A

34

8

17

R396

55

Golomane

41

Halcyon Drift

R 56

41

43

R393

Maclear

21

25

Ntywenka

9

30

Zwelitsha

B

Barkly Pass

Ugie

Dyoki

5

Barkly Pass

21

49

15

22

27

Masibambane

Elliot

7

R 56

10

7

16

16

6

5

20

Cala Road

20

55

C

17

Qiba

20

Ku-Mayima

Calapas

Cala

R 58

45

Whitmore

Ntibane

Satansnek

R 61

All Saints Nek

Langdon

18

Engcobo

6

18

Coghlan

Tsazo

10

35

eXwili

Gcina

21

20

Mgwali

16

R 61

Clarkebury

Bityi

8

D

KwaMzola

32

N 2

12

8

78

13

Bashee

31

Nobokwe

Halane

Mabheleni

Malobeleni

Mamba

R408

Qokama

Garner's Drift

18

Ndlunkulu

Munyu

31° 00'

Umtata 72km

31° 30' Umtata 42km

Umtata 38km

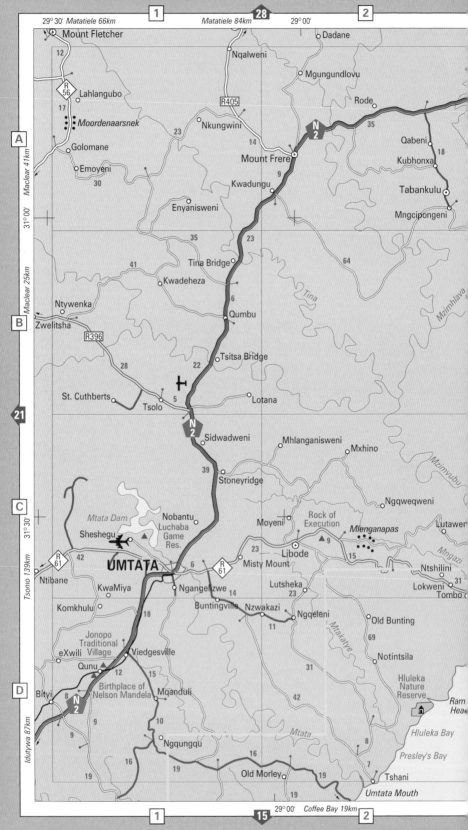

50km Kokstad 29° 30' **3** 50km Kokstad   **29**   **4** 30° 00' Harding 42 km

Oribi Gorge
Nat. Res.

Sipolweni 34   34   40   Mtamvuna   Nqabeni   **N2**

N2

Fort Donald   Kundayingana   Izingolweni   79

R394   **A**

Mount Ayliff   Nomlacu   Kwandunge   KwaZulu-Natal

Magusheni   18   Bizana   27

10   16   Redoubt

R61   31   40   Umtamvuna
Nature Reserve   Munster

Koloni   35   36

Port Edward

E a s t e r n   Banner Rest

36   Flagstaff   26   **C a p e**

Gabajana

11   Mtentu   **B**

Holy Cross   46

34   Umtentu

34   Mkambati
Nature Reserve

Palmerton   Dumesi   38   Mkambati

6   South Sand Bluff

Lusikisiki   Port Grosvenor

R61   19   Lambasi Bay

41   Mzintlava   Mbotyi   **C**

Gemvale   Manteku

R61   3

Imngazi
Mouth   Port St. Johns

Silaka Nature Reserve   **D**

Boulder Bay

SEE PAGES 108-111

I N D I A N

O C E A N

29° 30'   **3**   30° 00'   **4**

34km Port Shepstone

31°00' Port Shepstone 58km

31° 30'

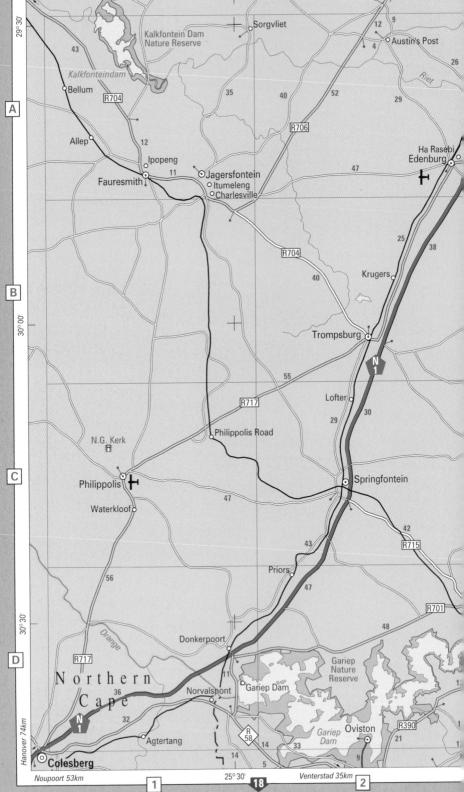

Koffiefontein 43km

25° 30'

Bloemfontein 60km

29° 30'

Sorgvliet

Kalkfontein Dam
Nature Reserve

12   9

4

Austin's Post

Kalkfonteindam

43

26

Bellum

35

40

52

29

Riet

R704

A

R706

12

Allep

Ipopeng

11

Jagersfontein

47

Ha Rasebi
Edenburg

Fauresmith

Itumeleng
Charlesville

25

38

R704

B

30° 00'

40

Krugers

Trompsburg

N
1

55

R717

Lofter

Philippolis Road

29

30

N.G. Kerk

C

Philippolis

Springfontein

47

42

Waterkloof

R715

43

56

Priors

47

R701

30° 30'

48

Donkerpoort

D

R717

Gariep
Nature
Reserve

Northern

1

Orange

11

Cape

36

Norvalspont

Gariep Dam

N
1

32

R390

R58

Oviston

21

Agtertang

14

33

9

Hanover 74km

Colesberg

14

5

Noupoort 53km

25° 30'

18

Venterstad 35km

26° 00' *Bloemfontein 40km* |3| *Bloemfontein 31km* 26° 30' |4| *Bloemfontein 36km*

29° 30'

N1

18

N6

42 35 10 Meadows 31

16 Dewetsdorp Morojaneng 14

Qhoweng Reddersburg R717 **A**

Rietwater 52 21km Wepener 75km

17 R717 26

37

39

Wolwepoort **B**

30° 00'

74 75

Gomvlei R701

72 **N6** **26**

F r e e S t a t e

Breipaal Caledon

16 Smithfield **C**

R701 39

Dupleston 43

36 Zastron 40km

Louw Wepener 20 Rouxville

10 Tussen-die-Rivier 27 Koukraal SEE PAGES 94-99 **N6**

Pellissier House and Museum Game Farm 30° 30'

Bethulie Goedemoed **D**

15 34 34

8 8 18 14

E a s t e r n 14 14

14 13 11 8 14

C a p e 5 6 10 Hot Sulphur Springs

4 Dukathole **Aliwal North**

9 Knapdaar 12 7 6 R58 16 19

26° 00' |3| *Burgersdorp* **19** *57km* 26° 30' |4| *Queenstown 163km*

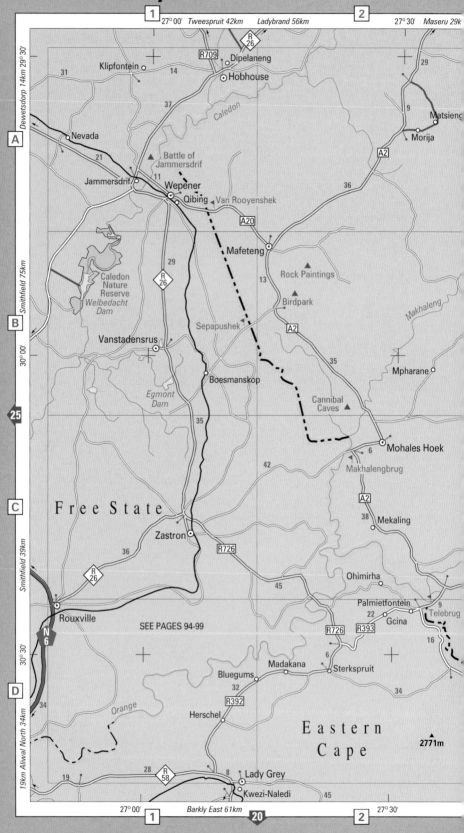

R709
R26
Dipelaneng
Klipfontein
14
Hobhouse
29
31
37
9
Matsieng
Caledon
Morija
Nevada
A2
A
21
Battle of
Jammersdrif
36
11
Jammersdrif
Wepener
Qibing
Van Rooyenshek
A20
Dewetsdorp 14km 29° 30'
Mafeteng
Rock Paintings
29
13
R26
Birdpark
*Caledon
Nature
Reserve*
*Welbedacht
Dam*
Sepapushek
A2
Makhaleng
B
Smithfield 75km
30° 00'
Vanstadensrus
Mpharane
35
Boesmanskop
*Egmont
Dam*
Cannibal
Caves
25
35
Mohales Hoek
6
Makhalengbrug
42
A2
38
Mekaling
C
F r e e   S t a t e
Zastron
36
R726
Ohimirha
45
Palmietfontein
9
R26
22
Telebrug
Rouxville
R726
R393
Gcina
16
N6
SEE PAGES 94–99
6
Smithfield 39km
30° 30'
Madakana
Bluegums
Sterkspruit
34
D
32
R392
34
Herschel
**E a s t e r n
C a p e**
Orange
2771m
19km Aliwal North 34km
34
28
R58
8
Lady Grey
19
Kwezi-Naledi
45

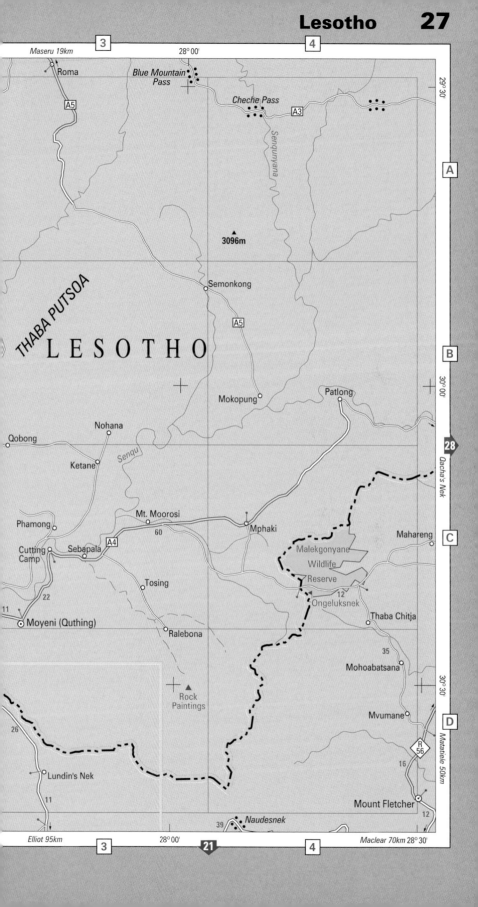

Maseru 19km

28° 00'

Roma

Blue Mountain
Pass

Cheche Pass

A5

A3

Senqunyana

29° 30'

A

▲
3096m

Semonkong

THABA PUTSOA

A5

L E S O T H O

30° 00'

B

Mokopung

Patlong

Nohana

Qobong

Senqu

28

Ketane

Qacha's Nek

Phamong

Mt. Moorosi

Mphaki

Mahareng

C

60

Cutting
Camp

Sebapala

A4

Malekgonyane
Wildlife
Reserve

Tosing

12

Ongeluksnek

Thaba Chitja

22

11

35

Moyeni (Quthing)

Ralebona

Mohoabatsana

30° 30'

Rock
Paintings

Mvumane

D

26

R
56

16

Matatiele 50km

Lundin's Nek

11

Mount Fletcher

12

39

Naudesnek

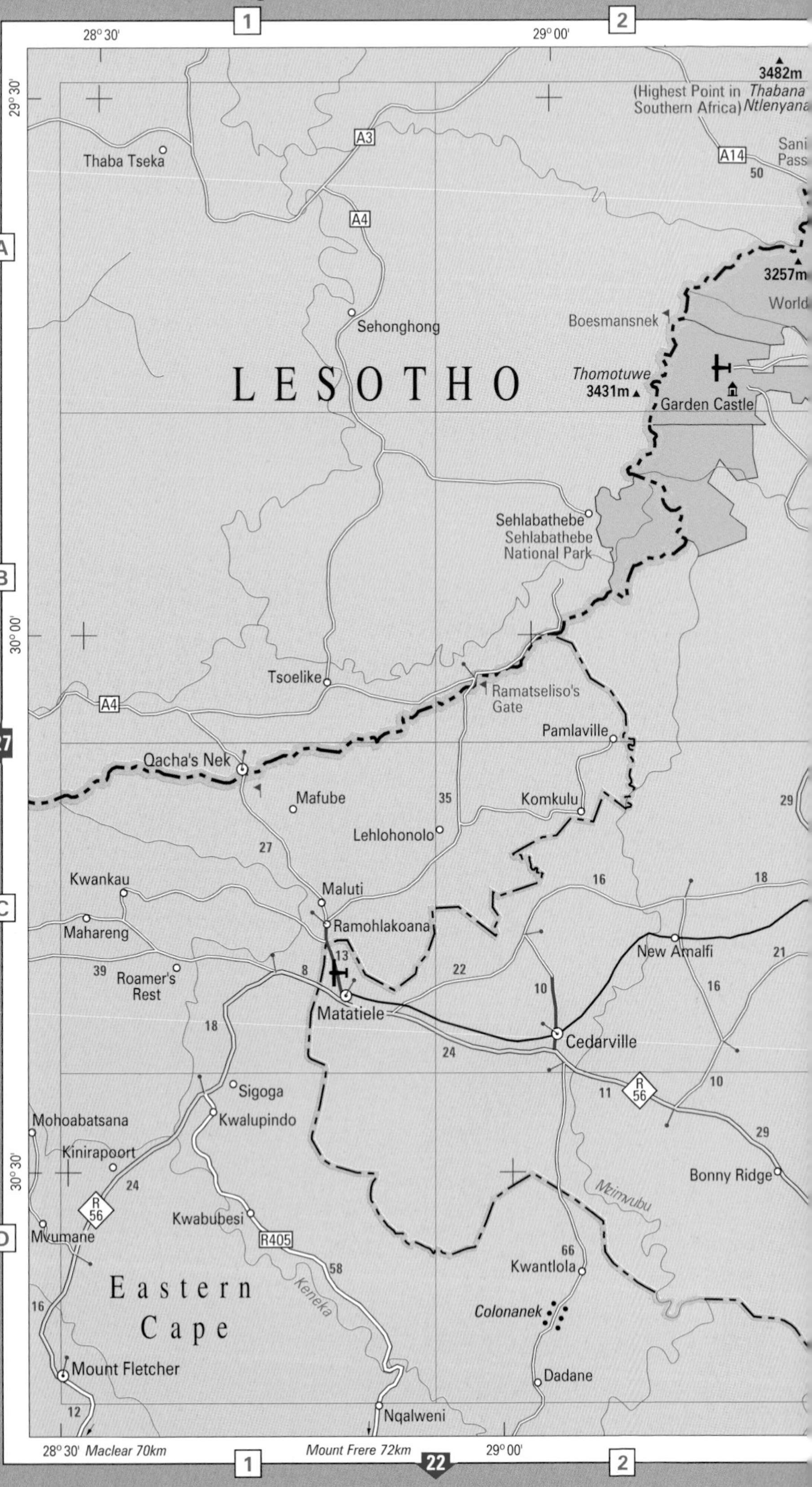

Map grid references

28° 30'
29° 00'

29° 30'

1
2

3482m ▲
(Highest Point in *Thabana*
Southern Africa) *Ntlenyana*

A3

Thaba Tseka

A14
50

A4

3257m ▲

World

A

Sehonghong

Boesmansnek

L E S O T H O

Thomotuwe
3431m ▲
Garden Castle

Sehlabathebe
Sehlabathebe
National Park

B

30° 00'

Tsoelike

Ramatseliso's
Gate

A4

Pamlaville

27

Qacha's Nek

Komkulu

29

Mafube

35

Kwankau

Lehlohonolo

16

18

C

Maluti

Mahareng

Ramohlakoana

New Amalfi

21

39
Roamer's
Rest

8
13

22

16

18

Matatiele

10

Cedarville

24

Sigoga

11
R
56

10

Mohoabatsana

Kwalupindo

29

Kinirapoort

Mzimvubu

Bonny Ridge

30° 30'

24

R
56

Mvumane

Kwabubesi

R405

D

66

58

Kwantlola

Keneka

*E a s t e r n
C a p e*

Colonanek

16

12

Mount Fletcher

Dadane

Nqalweni

28° 30' *Maclear 70km*

Mount Frere 72km

22

29° 00'

1

2

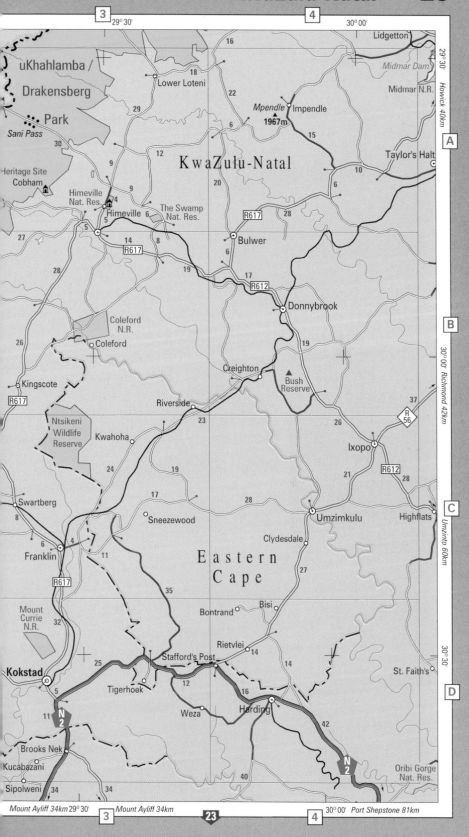

uKhahlamba /
Drakensberg
Park

Sani Pass

Lidgetton

Midmar Dam

Midmar N.R.

Lower Loteni

Mpendle Impendle
1967m

Taylor's Halt

KwaZulu-Natal

Heritage Site
Cobham

Himeville
Nat. Res.
Himeville

The Swamp
Nat. Res.

R617

R617

Bulwer

R612

Donnybrook

Coleford
N.R.
Coleford

Kingscote

R617

Creighton

Bush
Reserve

Riverside

Ntsikeni
Wildlife
Reserve

Kwahoha

R 56

Ixopo

R612

Swartberg

Sneezewood

Umzimkulu

Highflats

E a s t e r n
C a p e

Clydesdale

Franklin

R617

Bontrand

Bisi

Rietvlei

Mount
Currie
N.R.

Kokstad

Stafford's Post

St. Faith's

Tigerhoek

Weza

Harding

N
2

Brooks Nek

Kucabazani

Sipolweni

Oribi Gorge
Nat. Res.

N
2

Howick 40km

Richmond 42km

Umzinto 60km

30° 00'

30° 30'

Tourist Regions Tourist Regior

42	Tourist region maps and town plans
32	Chapter opener maps
◉	Point of interest

Langkloof Mountains near Port Elizabeth.

Swing bridge, Storms River mouth.

Eastern Beach, East London.

N1

Colesberg

N10   N9

Northern Cape

N1   R56

Richmond   79 Middelburg

Graaff-Reinet Area Map
70-73

Western Cape

R63

Karoo Heartland 68   77

78 Graaff-Reinet   Cradoc

Mountain Zebra National Park

Karoo Nature Reserve   74-75

Pearston 80

N9

R63

R75   81 Somerset East

Sundays River Valley
48-51

Addo Elepha National Par

Sundays River Valley

Baviaanskloof Wilderness Areas

R62   Joubertina 36   Jeffreys Bay   67 Uitenhage

Kareedouw 37   59   62-63 PORT ELIZABETH

N2

Tsitsikamma National Park
34-35   Humansdorp   Summerstran

58   65

32 Tsitsikamma   St Francis Bay
66   St Francis Bay Area Map
46-47

ourist Regions Tourist Regions

LESOTHO

Underberg
R612

N6

KwaZulu-Natal

Aliwal North 100
R58

R391

Barkly East 101

R56

Kokstad

N2

Mount Ayliff

R61

Port Edward

Burgersdorp 102

92 Friendly N6

103 Dordrecht

R56 Elliot 104
R58

113 UMTATA

R61

Port St Johns
112

Friendly N6 Area Map
94-99

R61

N2

Queenstown
105

N2

106
Wild Coast

N6

84-87
Amatola-Hogsback

Cathcart 88

82 Amatola Mountains

Wild Coast
108-111

aide 76

Stutterheim 91

90 King William's Town

Bisho

R63

Gonubie 56

Fort Beaufort
89

Beacon Bay 53

61 Peddie

EAST LONDON
54-55

Fishermen at East London.

ari

Grahamstown
57

R72

N2

Port Alfred 64

andria Kenton-on-Sea
60

38 Sunshine Coast & Country

Settler Country
40-45

INDIAN OCEAN

Town Hall, Graaff-Reinet.

Tsitsikamma Tsitsikamma Tsit

The Tsitsikamma is a breathtaking stretch of the Garden Route filled with natural drama: majestic mountain ranges, deep river gorges and jam-packed forests all seem to spill out into the wave-crunched rocky coastline. The natural beauty here is one of a kind, with a surfeit of indigenous animals and birds, mostly living between the magnificent indigenous yellowwoods and unique fynbos. Adventurers can take their pick of blackwater tubing down the Storms River, staring down the barrel of the world's largest bungee jump (on Bloukrans Bridge), hiking the Otter Trail or the more leisurely pursuit of picking fruit in the nearby Langkloof Valley. The San people first called this area the 'place of sparkling waters'.

LANGKLOOF VALLEY

Take a scenic drive through fruit orchards in season.
See the wonderful views in this valley known as the 'Valley of a Thousand Vistas'.
Visit the Langkloof Cheese Factory where you can also sample black olives.
The Formosa Peak Trail takes you to the highest natural beacon in the Tsitsikamma Mountains.
Other activities include mountain biking, 4X4 trails, angling and microlighting.

TSITSIKAMMA NATIONAL PARK

Bungee jump from the Bloukrans Bridge.
Hike the Otter Trail.
Take a guided tour through the Tsitsikamma Forest.
Abseil down the Storms River Gorge.
Go on an eco-adventure cruise to view the Storms River Gorge.

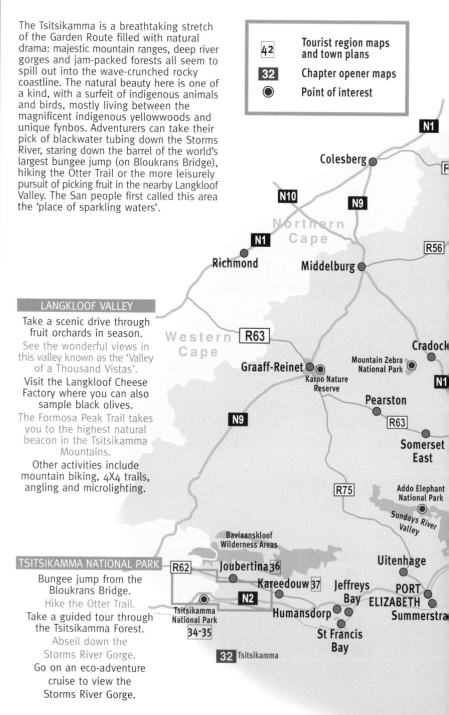

42	Tourist region maps and town plans
32	Chapter opener maps
◉	Point of interest

Underberg

R612

ree
ate

N6

Aliwal North

R58

R391

Burgersdorp

Barkly East

LESOTHO

KwaZulu-
Natal

R56

Kokstad

N2

Mount
Ayliff

R61

Port
Edward

Dordrecht

R56

Elliot

R58

UMTATA

R61

Port St Johns

Queenstown

R61

N2

N6

Cathcart

Stutterheim

aide

King William's
Town

Fort
Beaufort

R63

Bisho

Gonubie
Beacon Bay
EAST LONDON

ari

Peddie

Grahamstown

R72

xandria

Port Alfred
Kenton-on-Sea

INDIAN
OCEAN

Hiking trail, Tsitsikamma.

Joubertina 13km

Port Elizabeth 181km

34° 00'

34° 00'

23° 45'

23° 45'

23° 30'

23° 30'

A

B

C

D

E

Krakeelrivier 13

Krakee

Krakeel

Die Hoek

Vryheid

Formosa Peak
1676m

Louterwater

Appledale

Many Waters

Soetkraal

Dwars

Groot

Bobbejaan

Lottering

Bloukrans

Bloukrans
749m

R62

55

Avontuur 55km

Eastern Cape

Elandsbos

Lottering

Coldstream

Big Tree

Ragbos

R102

N2

Otter

Oakhurst Hut

Scott's
Hut

Tsitsikamma National Park

Robsloep

Khoisan Village

Bloukrans

Bloukrans Bridge
Bungi

Clinton's
Bank

Soutstrand

Bloukrans Pass

Platbos

Covie

Grootkloof

Grootrivier Pass

Die Punt

Skuinsbank

The Vlassot
Tsitsikamma Rest Camp

INDIAN OCEAN

TSITSIKAMMA
TOLL ROAD

Honeyhills

Heidehof

R102

13

Witberg
1134m

Tsitsikamma
National
Park

Kurland

Monkeyland

Arch Rock

Arch Rock

Kurland

West Cottage
Forrest Hall

Keurboomstrand

The Crags

N2

Brackenburn

Arch Rock

Redford

Matjies River Cave

Dune Park

Keurbooms

Little Crags

Keurboom
River
Nature
Reserve

Whiskey Creek
Nature Reserve

Aventura Eco
Plettenberg

Hangklip

Western Cape

Spitskop
627m

Boplaas

Keurbooms

R340

Wittedrif

Plettenberg Bay 8km

N

Scale 1 : 225 000

6km

4

2

0

4 Kareedouw 30km **5** Humansdorp 56km 34° 00' **6**

T S I T S I K A M M A B E R G E

Witels

Jagersbos
Jagersbos
Jagersbos
Draaiklip
Kammiebos
Onderplaas
Kompanjiesdrif
R 62 30
Vlakte
Uitkyk
Krugersland
Krugerskraal
Mooiplaas
Heights
Nooitrus
Wyekloof
Dennehoek

Joubertina 12km
Twee Riviere
24° 00'

Ouebosrand
Oudebosch
Boplaas
Protea
Far'n away
Ouebosstrand
R102
18
13
7

Groot
Witelsbos
Green Pastures
Hillcrest
Voëlkrans
Tsitsikamma
National Park

N2

Wit-Elskop
1251m

Elands
Saalrus
5
Witels
3
Tsitsikamma
Cottages
Guest House

Kruis
Tsitsikamma
Lodge
4
H
Sanddrif

Sanddrif
Blue Lillies Bush
Dolphin View &
Misty Mountain
Tannenhof
Fernery
Forest Ferns
Platbank

24° 00'
C

Skuinsbaai

IN STORMS RIVER
Ploughmans Rest
Rainbow Lodge
Storms River Guest House
Tranquility Woodcutters Cottage

Storms
Thornham
Grasslands
Storms River
Bridge
Bush Pig &
Tree Fern
5
4
Storms River
Big Tree
Stormsriver
Pass
Dolphin
Storms River Mouth
Rest Camp
Suspension
Bridge
George's Bay
Skuitbaai

INDIAN OCEAN
D

N2
Tweerivertjies
Tweerivertjies
5
Witteklip
Stormsriver
Pass
Ngubu Hut
Wall Point

Jerling

Kleinbos
Kleinbos
Otter
Scott's
Hut
Elandsbos
7
Tsitsikamma
National Park
E

IN STORMS RIVER
Armagh
Old Village Inn
H

Tsitsikamma

4 **5** Plettenberg Bay 34 53km 34° 00' **6**

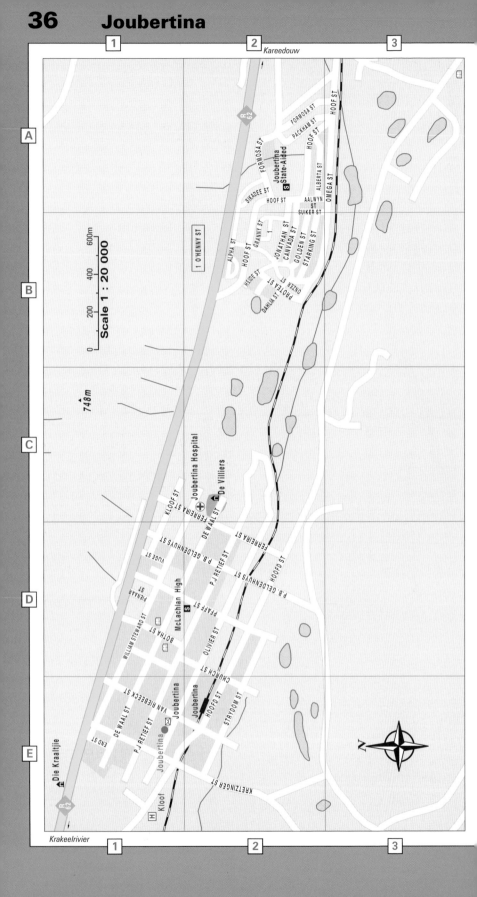

Kareedouw

1   2   3

600m
400
200
0

Scale 1 : 20 000

1 O'HENNY ST

R62

A

FORMOSA ST
FORMOSA ST
PACKHAM ST
HOOF ST
HOOF ST
HOOF ST
Joubertina
State-Aided
ALBERT ST
OMEGA ST
SIKADEE ST
HOOF ST
AALWYN ST
SUIKER ST

ALPHA ST
HOOF ST
GRANNY ST
HEIDE ST
JONATHAN ST
CANVADA ST
GOLDEN ST
STARKING ST
ONZER ST
PROTEA ST
DAHLIA ST
WILWIG ST

B

748m

C

KLOOF ST
Joubertina Hospital
FERREIRA ST
DE WAAL ST
De Villiers
FERREIRA ST
HOOF ST

VUGE ST
P.B. GELDENHUYS ST
P.J RETIEF ST
P.B GELDENHUYS ST
HOOF ST

D

PIENAAR ST
McLachlan High
PFAFF ST
OLIVIER ST
WILLIAM STEWARD ST
BOTHA ST
CHURCH ST

DE WAAL ST
VAN RIEBEECK ST
P.J RETIEF ST
Joubertina
Joubertina
HOOFD ST
STRYDOM ST
END ST
Joubertina

E

Die Kraaltjie
R62
Kloof
KRETZINGER ST

N

Krakeelrivier

1   2   3

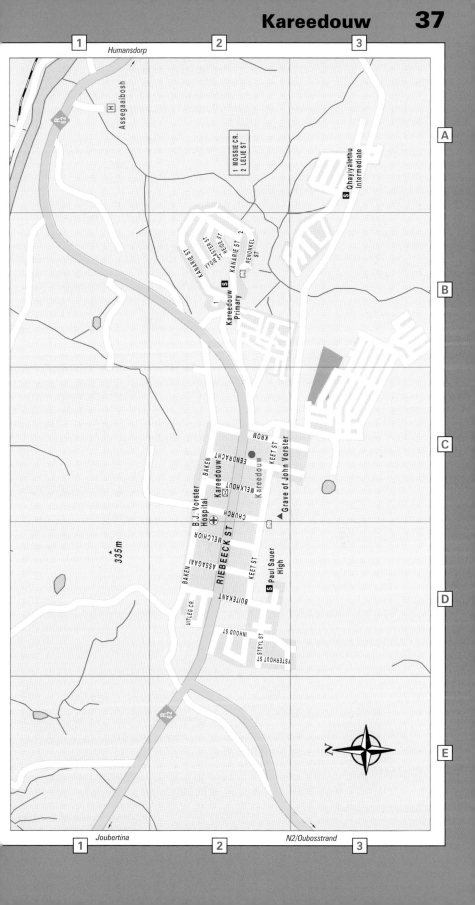

Sunshine Coast & Country Su

The Sunshine Coast is a hive of sun, fun and water activities, with hundreds of kilometres of magnificent unspoilt beaches that lay claim to the greatest number of sunshine hours along South Africa's entire coastline. Slightly inland, there are hundreds of thousands of hectares of malaria-free game reserves, notably the esteemed Addo Elephant National Park. Addo's 'tusky citizens' have swelled in number from around a dozen in the 1930s to over 300 today, most of whom can be relatively easily seen in their largely flat environment. Port Elizabeth (aka The Friendly City) is the perfect big city base for explorers, with beaches, nature, facilities and history all in abundance and within touching distance, while inland Grahamstown is a student town that has charm by the truckload, as well as bucketfuls of historical sites and memorials.

42	Tourist region maps and town plans
32	Chapter opener maps
◉	Point of interest

GRAHAMSTOWN

See the best of local and imported talent at the National Arts Festival in July each year. This is the home of the world renowned Rhodes University. See the many places of worship in this town that is also known as 'the city of saints'. Visit museums housing collections that focus on the history of conflict between the Xhosa and British.

PORT ELIZABETH

Bayworld is a must-see offering a museum, oceanarium, snakepark and tropical house. Take a ride on the famous narrow gauge steam train leaving from PE and crossing Van Staden's bridge (the world's highest narrow gauge bridge). Visit the cultural village of 'Kaya Lendaba', a unique living village situated next to Shamwari Game Reserve. Activities include golf, fishing, hiking, horse riding, watersports, game viewing, cycling and birding.

N1

Colesberg

N10

N9

Northern Cape

N1

R56

Richmond

Middelburg

Western Cape

R63

Crado

Graaff-Reinet

Mountain Zebra National Park

Karoo Nature Reserve

N9

Pearston

R63

R75

Somerset East

Sundays River Valley
48-51

Addo Eleph National P

Sundays River Valley

Baviaanskloof Wilderness Areas

R62

Joubertina

Kareedouw

Jeffreys Bay
59

67 Uitenhage

62-63 PORT ELIZABETH

N2

Tsitsikamma National Park

58 Humansdorp

Summerstrand
65

St Francis Bay
66

St Francis Bay Area Map
46-47

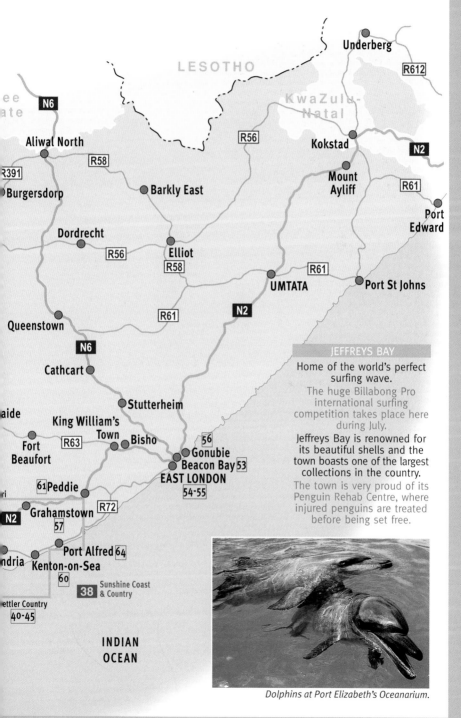

LESOTHO

KwaZulu-Natal

Underberg

R612

N6

R56

Kokstad

N2

Aliwal North

R58

Mount Ayliff

R61

R391

Burgersdorp

Barkly East

Port Edward

Dordrecht

R56

Elliot

R58

R61

UMTATA

Port St Johns

Queenstown

R61

N2

N6

Cathcart

Stutterheim

aide

King William's Town

Bisho

R63

Fort Beaufort

56

Gonubie

Beacon Bay 53

EAST LONDON

54-55

61 Peddie

Grahamstown

R72

57

N2

Port Alfred 64

ndria Kenton-on-Sea

60

38 Sunshine Coast & Country

ttler Country

40-45

INDIAN OCEAN

JEFFREYS BAY

Home of the world's perfect surfing wave.

The huge Billabong Pro international surfing competition takes place here during July.

Jeffreys Bay is renowned for its beautiful shells and the town boasts one of the largest collections in the country.

The town is very proud of its Penguin Rehab Centre, where injured penguins are treated before being set free.

Dolphins at Port Elizabeth's Oceanarium.

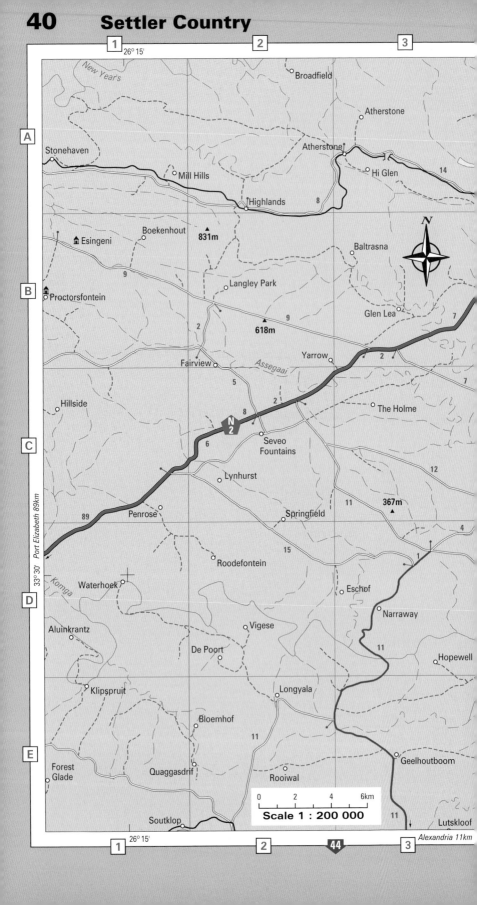

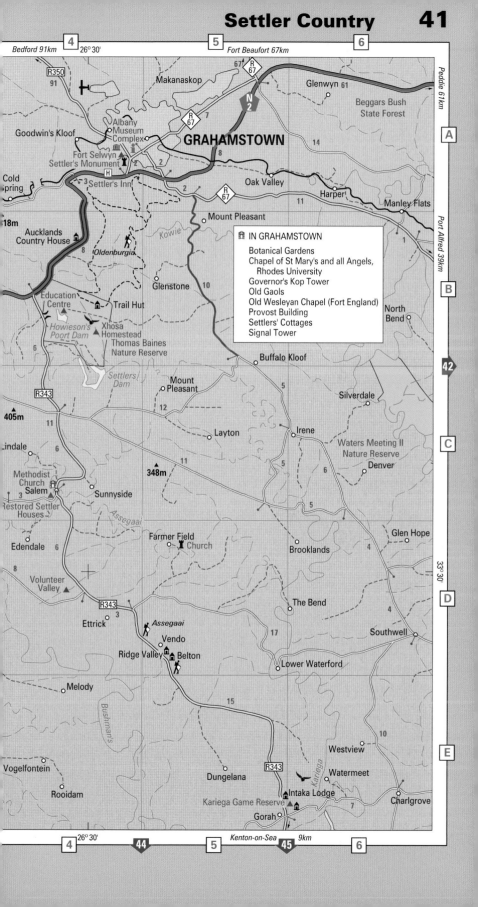

R350
91

Makanaskop

Glenwyn 61

Beggars Bush
State Forest

Albany
Museum
Complex

R67 7

N2

67

R67

Goodwin's Kloof

GRAHAMSTOWN

14

Fort Selwyn
Settler's Monument

Cold
Spring

3 Settler's Inn

Oak Valley

R67

Harper

Manley Flats

Mount Pleasant

11

Port Alfred 39km

18m

Aucklands
Country House

Kowie

1

North
Bend

Oldenburgia

Glenstone

10

Buffalo Kloof

Education
Centre

Trail Hut

Howieson's
Poort Dam

Xhosa
Homestead
Thomas Baines
Nature Reserve

Mount
Pleasant

5

Silverdale

IN GRAHAMSTOWN

Botanical Gardens
Chapel of St Mary's and all Angels,
  Rhodes University
Governor's Kop Tower
Old Gaols
Old Wesleyan Chapel (Fort England)
Provost Building
Settlers' Cottages
Signal Tower

42

Settlers
Dam

12

R343

405m

11

Layton

Irene

Waters Meeting II
Nature Reserve

Denver

Lindale

6

11

348m

5

6

Methodist
Church

Salem

3

Sunnyside

Assegaai

5

5

Restored Settler
Houses

Edendale

6

Farmer Field

Church

Brooklands

Glen Hope

8

Volunteer
Valley

R343

3

The Bend

4

Southwell

Ettrick

Assegaai

Vendo

17

Ridge Valley

Belton

Lower Waterford

Melody

15

Bushman's

Westview

10

Vogelfontein

R343

Dungelana

Kariega

Watermeet

Rooidam

Intaka Lodge

Charlgrove

Kariega Game Reserve

Gorah

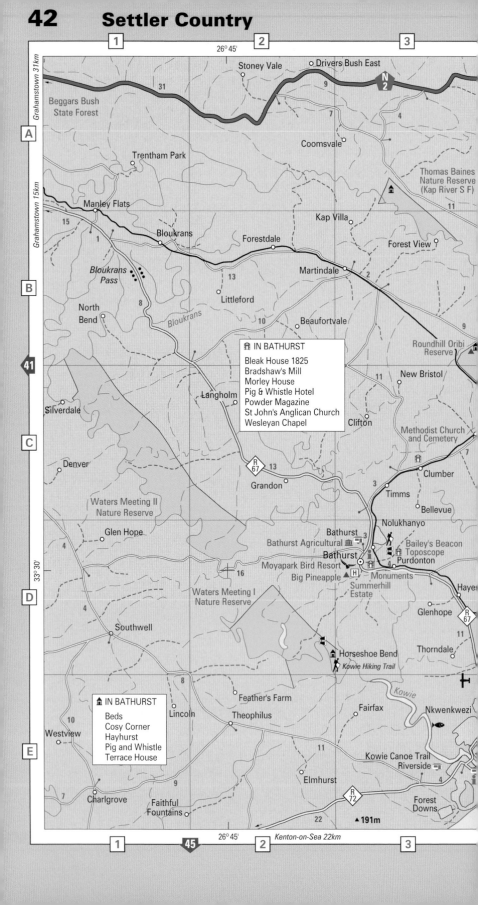

IN BATHURST
Bleak House 1825
Bradshaw's Mill
Morley House
Pig & Whistle Hotel
Powder Magazine
St John's Anglican Church
Wesleyan Chapel

IN BATHURST
Beds
Cosy Corner
Hayhurst
Pig and Whistle
Terrace House

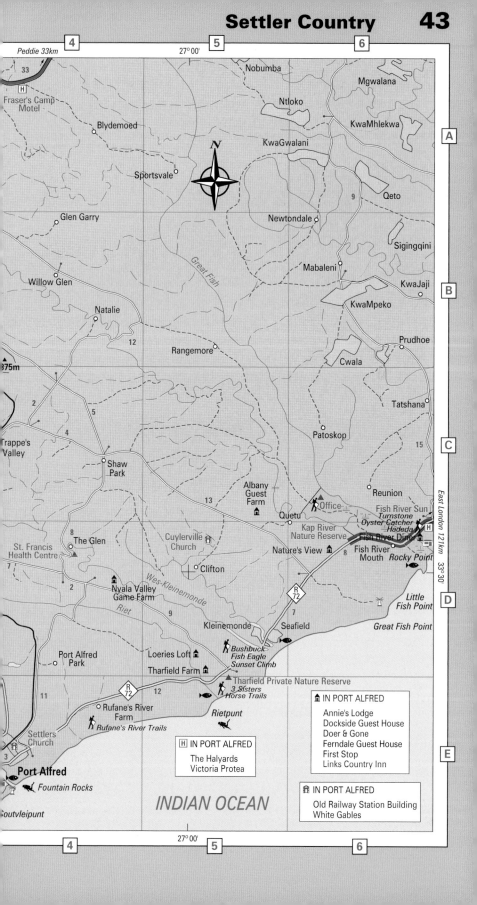

Peddie 33km

4 27° 00' **5** **6**

33

Fraser's Camp Motel

Nobumba

Ntloko

Mgwalana

KwaMhlekwa

Blydemoed

KwaGwalani

A

Sportsvale

Qeto

N

Glen Garry

Newtondale

Sigingqini

Mabaleni

Great Fish

KwaJaji

Willow Glen

B

KwaMpeko

Natalie

Prudhoe

12

Rangemore

Cwala

Tatshana

2

Trappe's Valley

Patoskop

15

5

C

4

Shaw Park

875m

Albany Guest Farm

Reunion

13

Fish River Sun

8

Office

Turnstone

Oyster Catcher

The Glen

Quetu

Kap River Nature Reserve

Hadeda

Fish River Diner

St. Francis Health Centre

Cuylerville Church

Nature's View

Fish River Mouth

Rocky Point

7

Clifton

8

Wes-Kleinemonde

Little Fish Point

D

2

Nyala Valley Game Farm

Riet

9

R 72

Great Fish Point

Kleinemonde

Seafield

7

Port Alfred Park

Loeries Loft

Bushbuck Fish Eagle Sunset Climb

11

Tharfield Farm

Tharfield Private Nature Reserve

R 72

12

3 Sisters Horse Trails

Rufane's River Farm

Rietpunt

Rufane's River Trails

Settlers Church

3

H IN PORT ALFRED
The Halyards
Victoria Protea

E

Port Alfred

Fountain Rocks

Boutvleipunt

IN PORT ALFRED
Annie's Lodge
Dockside Guest House
Doer & Gone
Ferndale Guest House
First Stop
Links Country Inn

IN PORT ALFRED
Old Railway Station Building
White Gables

INDIAN OCEAN

East London 121km

33° 30'

4 27° 00' **5** **6**

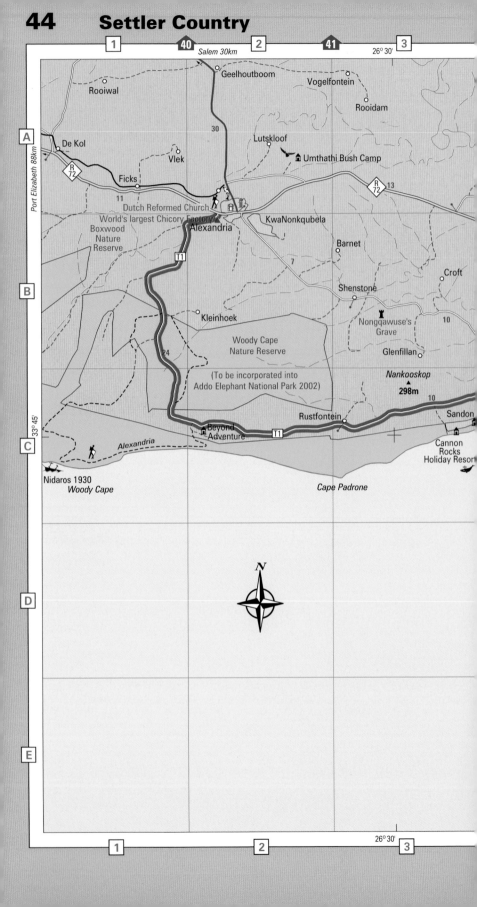

Salem 30km

26° 30'

Port Elizabeth 88km

Rooiwal
Geelhoutboom
Vogelfontein
Rooidam

A

De Kol
Vlek
Lutskloof
Umthathi Bush Camp

R72
Ficks
30

11
R72 13

Dutch Reformed Church
KwaNonkqubela

World's largest Chicory Factory
Alexandria
Boxwood
Nature
Reserve
Barnet

B

T1
Shenstone
Croft

Kleinhoek
Nongqawuse's
Grave
10

Woody Cape
Nature Reserve
Glenfillan

24
Nankooskop
298m

(To be incorporated into
Addo Elephant National Park 2002)
10

Rustfontein
Sandon

C

Beyond
Adventure
T1
Cannon
Rocks
Holiday Resort

Alexandria

Nidaros 1930
Woody Cape
Cape Padrone

33° 45'

D

N

E

26° 30'

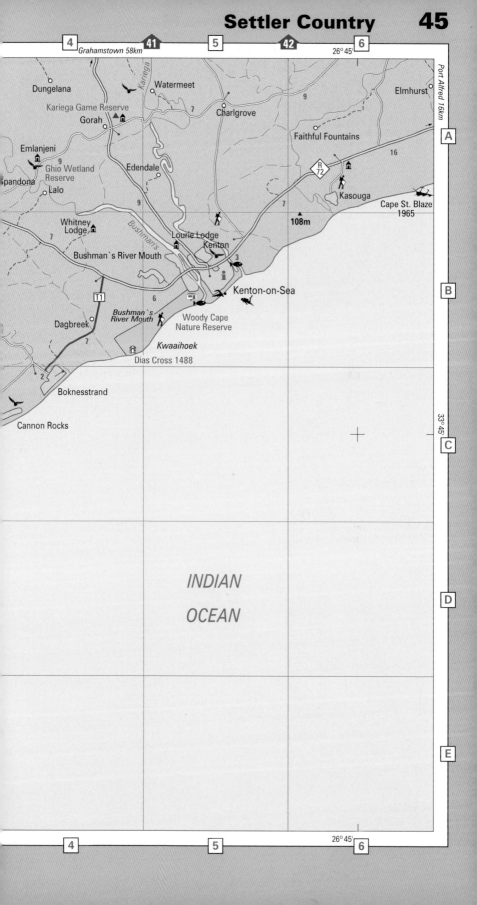

Port Alfred 16km

Dungelana

Watermeet

Elmhurst

Kariega Game Reserve

Gorah

Charlgrove

9

Faithful Fountains

A

Emlanjeni

Ghio Wetland Reserve

Edendale

R 72

16

Spandona

Lalo

Kasouga

Cape St. Blaze 1965

Bushman's

7

108m

Whitney Lodge

Lourie Lodge

Kenton

7

Bushman's River Mouth

3

i

T1

6

Kenton-on-Sea

B

Dagbreek

Bushman's River Mouth

Woody Cape Nature Reserve

Kwaaihoek

7

Dias Cross 1488

2

Boknesstrand

Cannon Rocks

33° 45'

C

INDIAN

OCEAN

D

E

1 2 3

34° 00'

Port Elizabeth 68km

Port Elizabeth 63km

Port Elizabeth 56km

Hankey 30km

Plettenberg Bay 56km

A

B

C

D

E

24° 50'

Kabeljous Nat. Res.

Kabeljous River Mouth

Kabeljous Holiday Resort

Wavecrest

Noorskloofpunt

Jeffreys Bay

Jeffreys Bay

Foulkes Point

Pellsrus

Marina Martinique

Seekoeipunt

Seekoei River Mouth

Paradise Beach

Aston Bay

Aston Bay 31m

47m

Swart

Seekoeiriver Nat. Res.

26m

Seekoei

Soutvlei

49m

Soutvlei

43m

N2

68

63

R102

Swartrivier

N2

Uitsig

The Burns

Rondebos

R102

R330

The Glen

Grasmere

R330

Boskloof

Kariega Cultural Centre

30

R330

95m

68m

Humansdorp

Seekoei

N2

Kruisfontein

R102

Gravelridge

164

140m

56

Scale 1 : 110 000

0 1 2 3km

34° 00'

Knysna 164km

1 2 3

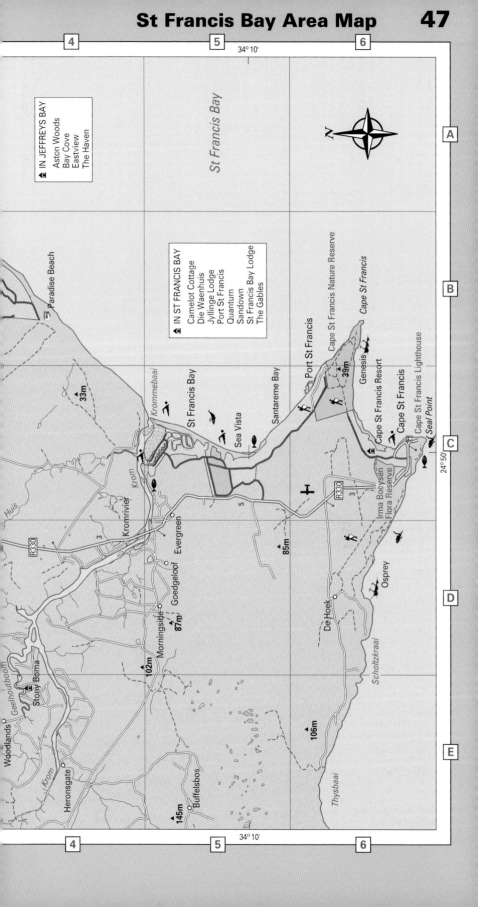

IN JEFFREYS BAY
Aston Woods
Bay Cove
Eastview
The Haven

IN ST FRANCIS BAY
Camelot Cottage
Die Waenhuis
Jyllinge Lodge
Port St Francis
Quantum
Sandown
St Francis Bay Lodge
The Gables

St Francis Bay

Paradise Beach

Krommebaai

St Francis Bay

Santareme Bay

Sea Vista

Port St Francis

Cape St Francis Nature Reserve

Cape St Francis

Genesis

39m

33m

Krom

Kromrivier

Goedgeloof

Evergreen

Morningside

Cape St Francis Resort

Cape St Francis

Cape St Francis Lighthouse

Seal Point

24° 50'

R330

R330

85m

87m

102m

106m

145m

Buffelsbos

Heronsgate

Woodlands

Stony Boma

Geelhoutboom

Huis

Krom

Imma Booysen
Flora Reserve

De-Hoek

Osprey

Scholtzkraal

Thysbaai

34° 10'

Jansenville 29km

1 **2** 25° 00' **3**

R75 29

A

Grootdam

Oslaagte

Waterford

12 R400

R400

10

5

Bloemhof

Tannies

8 Kwarrielaagte

Verskraal 13

Hurterskraal

B

26

11

Nel's Request

Stinkfontein

Gannahoek

Middelfontein

Koffielaagte

33° 15'

31

Scale 1 : 250 000

0 2 4 6 8km

R75 10

C

Pinelands

Vaalfontain

Hartebeesfontein

Old Koms

Springvale

Wolwefontein

54

Otjieskraal

Cauchassie

Steytlerville 54km

Vredenal

Waterplaas

6

Kleinpoort

Grootpoort

R75

Matjiesfontein

5

5

D

Cockscomb

Rockdale

Sapkamma

Grasvlakte

Paardenlaagte

19

Biesjevlei

Roodekrans

10

R75

12

Ghwarriekoppe

636m

Renosterhoek

Hillside

Rust en Vrede

E

Perserverance

Springbokflats

Brandkoppe

576m

Renosterhoek

1 **2** 25° 00' **3**

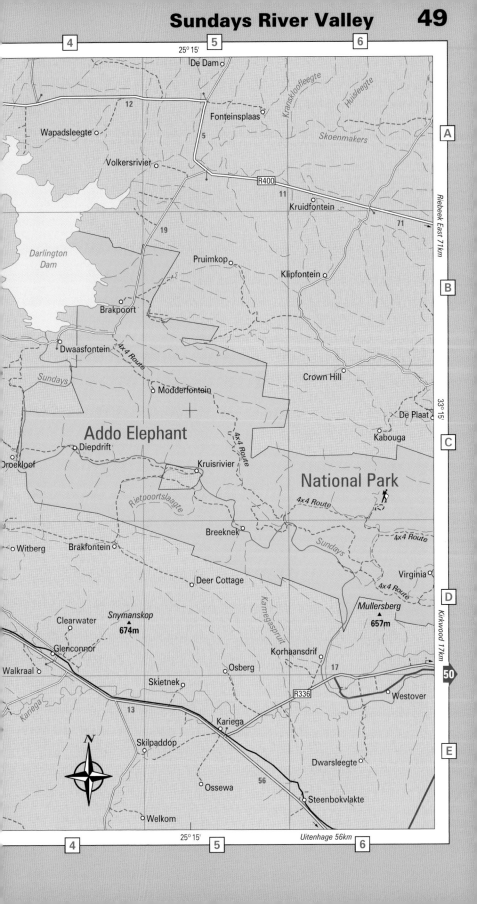

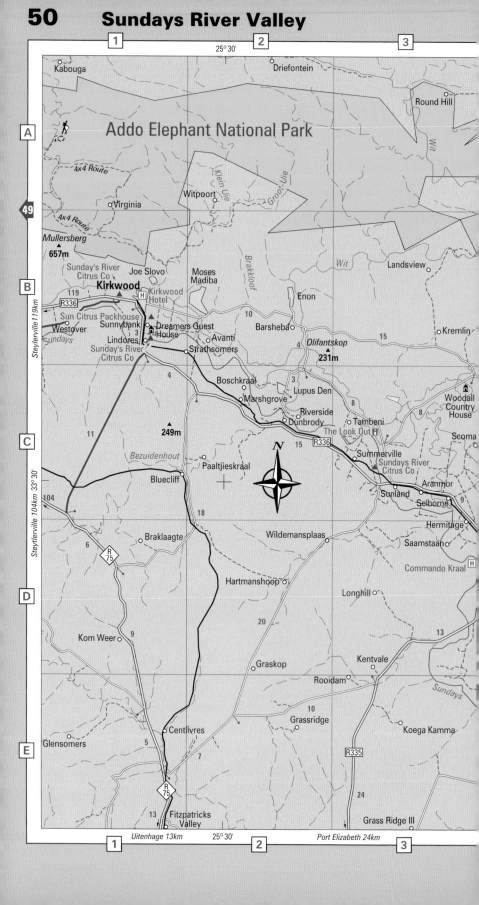

Kabouga

Driefontein

Round Hill

Addo Elephant National Park

4x4 Route

Witpoort

Virginia

Klein Uie

Groot-Uie

Wit

Landsview

4x4 Route

Mullersberg
▲ 657m

Sunday's River
Citrus Co

Joe Slovo

Moses
Madiba

Brakkloof

Wit

Kirkwood

Kirkwood
Hotel

Enon

Kremlin

119

R336

Sun Citrus Packhouse

Sunnybank

Westover

Lindores

Dreamers Guest
House

3

Sundays

Sunday's River
Citrus Co

Avanti

Strathsomers

10

Barsheba

15

4

Olifantskop
▲ 231m

Woodall
Country
House

4

Boschkraal

3

Lupus Den

8

Scoma

249m

Marshgrove

Riverside

Dunbrody

Tambeni

The Look Out

8

Bezuidenhout

Paaltjieskraal

15

R336

Summerville

Sundays River
Citrus Co

Aranmor

11

Bluecliff

Sunland

Selborne

9

104

Hermitage

18

Wildemansplaas

Saamstaan

Commando Kraal

6

R75

Braklaagte

Hartmanshoop

Longhill

Kom Weer

9

20

13

Graskop

Kentvale

Rooidam

Sundays

10

Grassridge

Koega Kamma

Centlivres

5

7

R335

Glensomers

R75

24

13

Fitzpatricks
Valley

Grass Ridge III

Steytlerville 119km   Steytlerville 104km 33° 30'

49

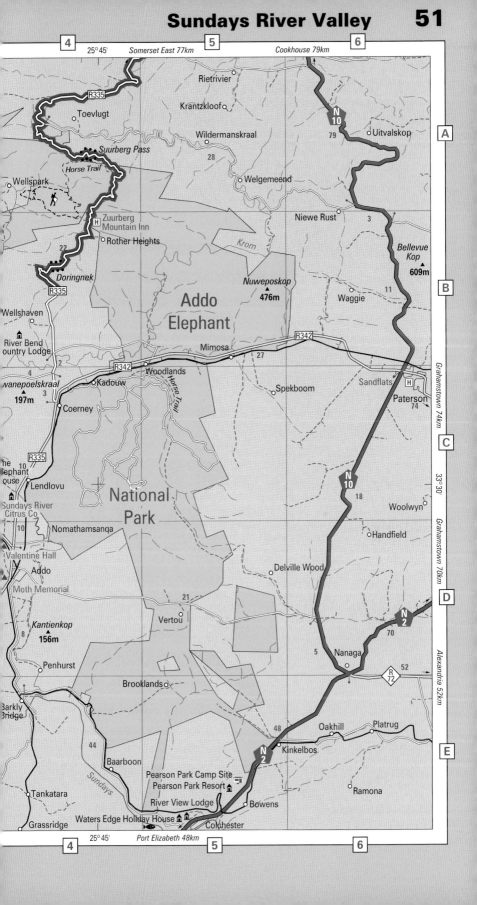

Rietrivier
Krantzkloof
Toevlugt
Wildermanskraal
R335
N10
79
Uitvalskop

A

Suurberg Pass
Horse Trail
Welgemeend
28

Wellspark

Zuurberg
Mountain Inn
Niewe Rust
3
Bellevue
Kop
609m

H

22
Rother Heights
Krom
Waggie
11

B

Doringnek
R335
Nuweposkop
476m

Wellshaven

**Addo
Elephant**

River Bend
Country Lodge
2
Mimosa
R342
27

nanepoelskraal
197m
R342
Woodlands
Spekboom
Sandflats
H
Paterson
74

4
3
Kadouw
Horse Trail

Coerney

C

R335
10
he
ephant
ouse
Lendlovu

N10
18
Woolwyn

**National
Park**

Sundays River
Citrus Co
10
Nomathamsanqa
Handfield

Valentine Hall
Addo
Delville Wood

Moth Memorial
21

Kantienkop
156m
Vertou

N2
70

D

8
5
Nanaga

Penhurst
R72
52

Brooklands

Barkly
Bridge
48
Oakhill
Platrug

44
Kinkelbos
N2

Baarboon
Pearson Park Camp Site
Pearson Park Resort
Ramona

E

Tankatara
Sundays
River View Lodge
Bowens

Grassridge
Waters Edge Holiday House
Colchester

Grahamstown 74km
33° 30'
Grahamstown 70km
Alexandria 52km

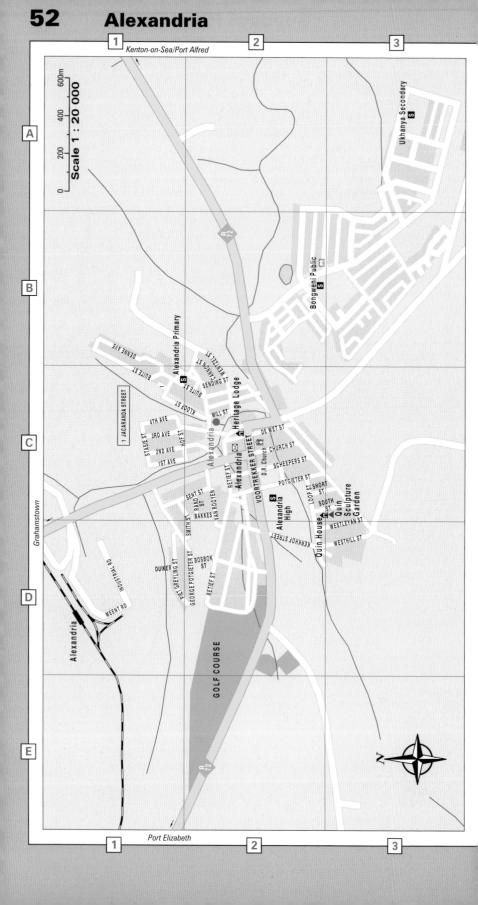

Scale 1 : 20 000

0   200   400   600m

Kenton-on-Sea/Port Alfred

Port Elizabeth

Ukhanya Secondary

Bongweni Public

R 72

DENNE AVE

BUITE ST

Alexandria Primary

KANON ST

VENTEL ST

SENDING ST

1 JACARANDA STREET

KLOOF ST

BUITE ST

MILL ST

Heritage Lodge

4TH AVE

3RD AVE

STASIE ST

2ND AVE

1ST AVE

HOF ST

Alexandria

DE WET ST

Alexandria

CHURCH ST

D.R. Church

RETIEF ST

VOORTREKKER STREET

SCHEEPERS ST

POTGIETER ST

Alexandria High

LOOP ST

SHORT ST

SOUTH ST

Quin Sculpture Garden

Quin House

WESTLEYAN ST

WESTHILL ST

KERKHOF STREET

SENT ST

RAND ST

BAKKES ST

SMITH ST

VAN ROOYEN

DUIKER ST

PIET GREYLING ST

GEORGE POTGIETER ST

BOSBOK ST

RETIEF ST

INDUSTRIAL RD

MEENT RD

Alexandria

GOLF COURSE

Grahamstown

R 72

N

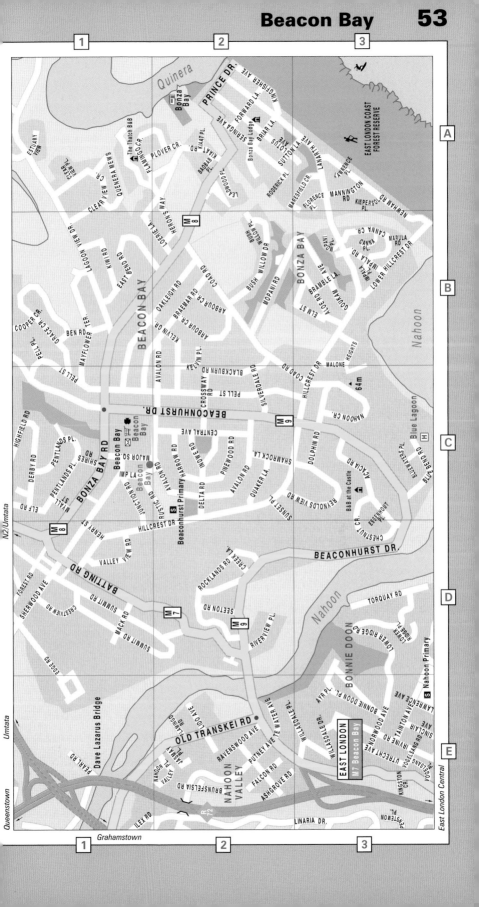

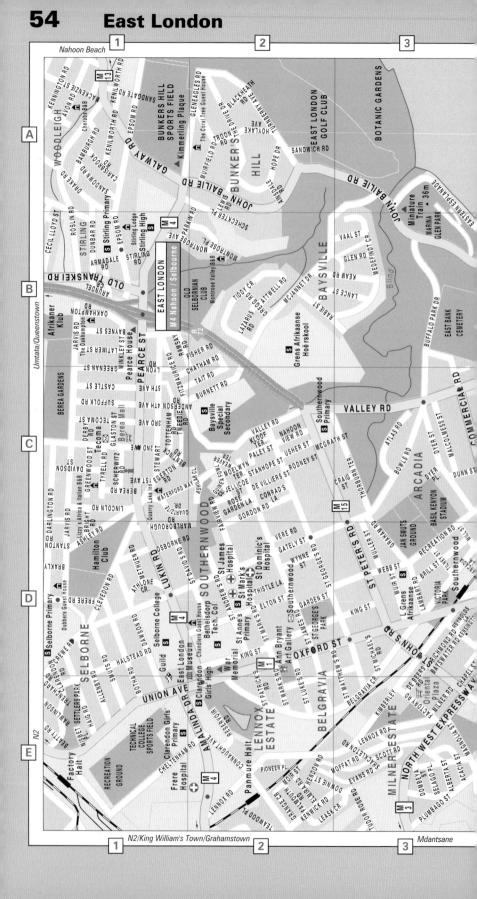

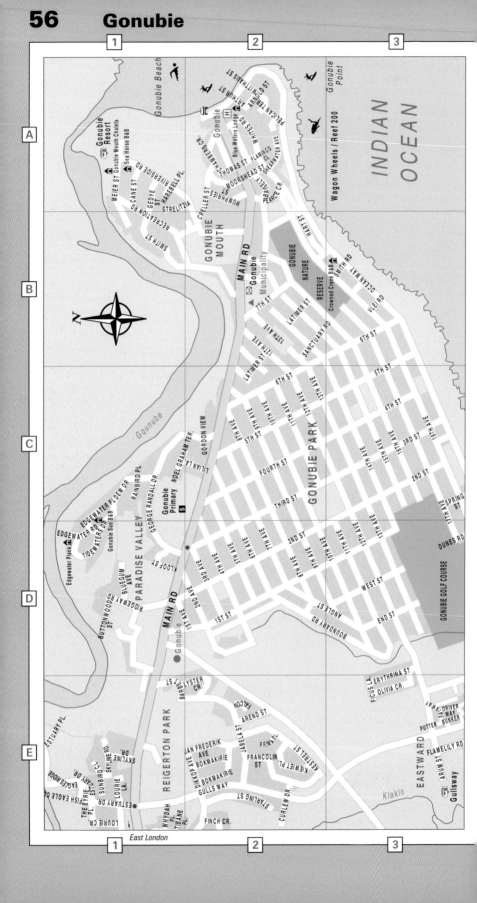

INDIAN OCEAN

Gonubie Point

Wagon Wheels / Reef 200

Gonubie Beach

Gonubie Resort
Gonubie Mouth Chalets
Sea Horse B&B
MEIER ST
RIVERSIDE RD
HAREBELL PL
GEDYE ST
CANE ST
RECREATION RD
STRELITZIA
SMITH ST
CRELLER ST
CHAMBERS CR.

GONUBIE MOUTH

Gonubie
Blue Waters Lodge
THOMAS ST
MOORSHEAD ST
HUMPHRIES ST
RITCHER ST
WITHERS RD
ARNOLD ST
PELICAN TERR
FLAMINGO CR.
SHEARWATER AVE
ISELY
PEARCE CR.

Gonubie Municipality
MAIN RD
7TH ST
13TH AVE
12TH AVE
LATIMER ST
LATIMER ST
HART ST
GONUBIE NATURE RESERVE
Crowned Crane B&B
SMITH RD
OCEAN WAY
VLEI RD
6TH ST
5TH ST
4TH ST
3RD ST
1ST ST
18TH AVE
SANCTUARY RD

Gqunube

EDGEWATER PL
PLOEN DR
RAMBIRD PL
EDGEWATER RD
Gonubie Surf B&B
TIDEWATERS DR
Edgewater Place
GORDON VIEW
NOEL GRAHAM TER.
LILIAN LA.
GEORGE RANDALL DR.
Gonubie Primary
KLOOF ST
6TH ST
8TH AVE
5TH AVE
9TH AVE
10TH AVE
11TH AVE
12TH AVE
13TH AVE
14TH AVE
15TH AVE
16TH AVE
2ND ST

GONUBIE PARK

FOURTH ST
THIRD ST
11TH AVE
SPRING ST
DUNES RD

BUTTONWOODS ST
RIDGEWAY RD
BLUEGUM AVE
PARADISE VALLEY
MAIN RD
Gonubie
1ST AVE
2ND AVE
3RD AVE
4TH AVE
5TH AVE
6TH AVE
7TH AVE
1ST ST
2ND ST
5TH AVE
6TH AVE
7TH AVE
8TH AVE
9TH AVE
10TH AVE
11TH AVE
12TH AVE
13TH AVE
THIRD ST
WEST ST
ANGLET ST
BOUNDARY RD
END ST

GONUBIE GOLF COURSE

ESTUARY PL.
EAGLES RIDGE
THE EYRIE
FISH EAGLE DR
SKYLINE RD
SUNBIRD CL.
SKYLINE DR.
LOURIE LA.
WHYDAH PL.
TIBANE PL.
ESTUARY DR.
LOURIE CR.
REIGERTON PARK
BARBET ST
LYSTER CR.
FALCON
AREND ST
JAN FREDERIK AVE
DIKKOP AVE
BOKMAKIRIE
BOKMAKIRIE
GULLS WAY
FINCH CR.
STARLING ST
CURLEW DR.
JABELA ST
KIEWIET PL.
P.R.N.V.
FRANCOLIN ST
KESTREL ST
FICUS LA.
ERYTHRINA ST
OLIVIA CR.
EASTWARD
FLAMELILY RD
ARUM ST
Gullsway
DRIVER WAY
PUTTER
BUNKER
Klaklo

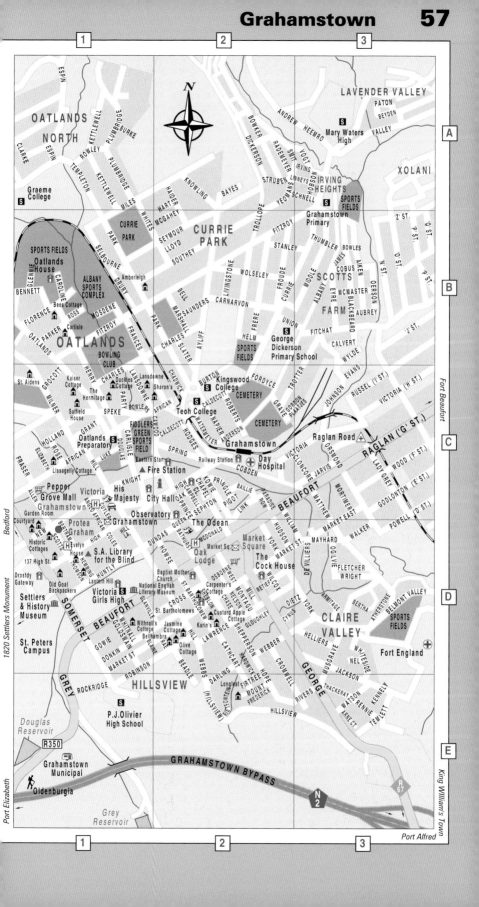

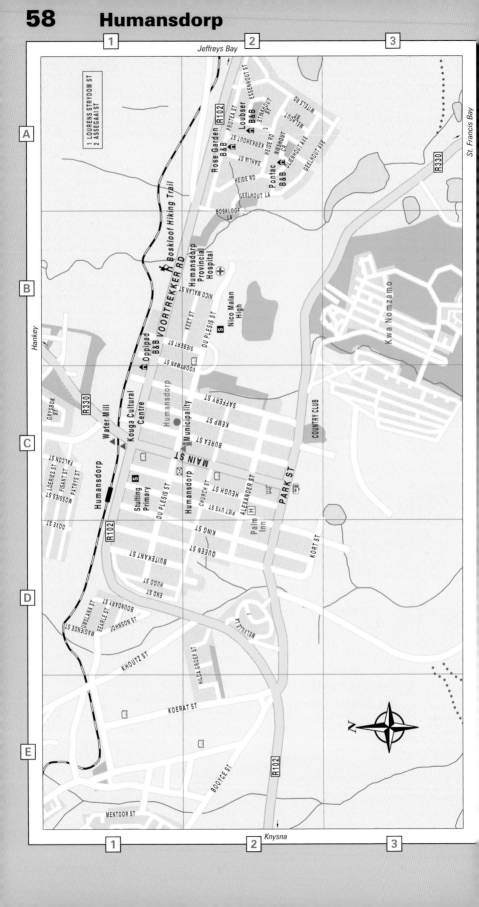

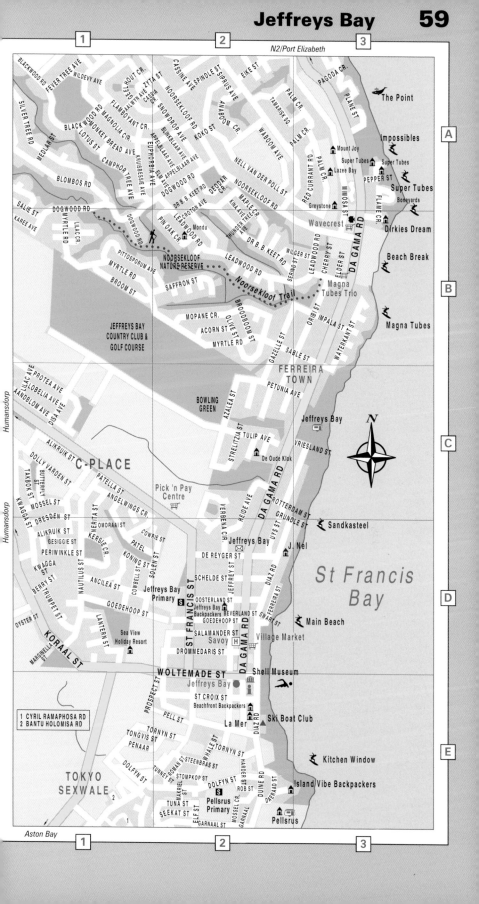

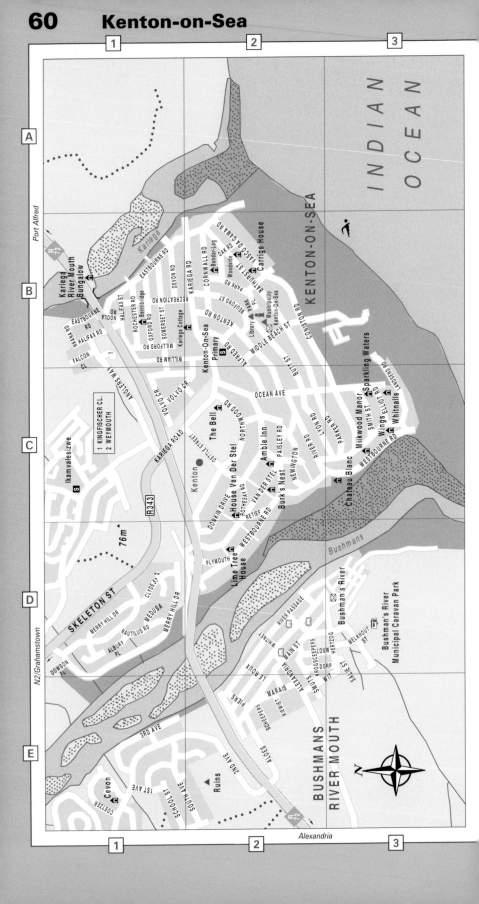

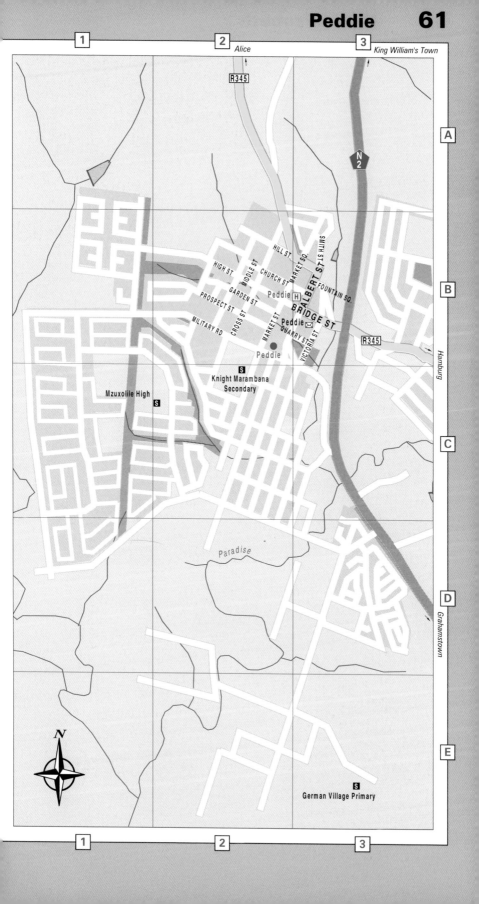

R345

N
2

Hamburg

R345

Grahamstown

HILL ST

HIGH ST

MIDDLE ST

CHURCH ST

MARKET SQ.

SMITH ST

ALBERT ST

FOUNTAIN SQ.

GARDEN ST

PROSPECT ST

CROSS ST

Peddie H

BRIDGE ST

MILITARY RD

MARKET ST

Peddie ⊠

QUARRY ST

VICTORIA ST

Peddie

Knight Marambana
Secondary

S

Mzuxolile High S

A

B

C

D

E

Paradise

N

German Village Primary S

Uitenhage
Swartkops Grahamstown/East London

PORT ELIZABETH
Mount Rd
M5

PORT ELIZABETH
Pell St Interchange
North End
Uitenhage Rd
Cape Town
Grahamstown
M54

North End

PORT ELIZABETH
Albany Rd Interchange
Albany Rd
M7

1 ANCHOR LA.
2 CONSTITUTION HILL
3 HOLLAND ST
4 JAMES ST

N

New Law Courts
DE VILLIERS ST
GATES ST
GRAHAM ST
BATES ST
HANCOCK ST
ROBERT ST
BRASSEL ST
TODD ST
PELL ST
DURBAN ST
ALICE ST
DOSSON ST
CHARLOTTE ST
ALBERT ST
DOYLE ST

Library
Excelsior Primary
Primary Health Clinic
North End
Grey Primary

EYRE ST
DIAZ RD
BOND ST
DE VILLIERS ST

MOUNT CROIX

HAZELHURST DR
ERITH ST
BAYVIEW AVE
NORTHWOOD RD
ATHLONE RD
CAMBRIDGE RD
JERSEY AVE

Erica Girls' Primary
TURVEY ST
HAZELHURST RD

Provincial Hospital
EASTBOURNE RD
CLEVEDON RD
WESTBOURNE RD

Victorian Houses
M7
NEWINGTON RD
DICKENS ST
BINGLEY ST

CAPE RD
Five Ways
KING GEORGES RD
ROSEBERRY LA.
PARK LA.
PARK DR.
UPPER DICKENS ST

Il King George's

ALBANY RD
ROCKAMAY ST
RICHMOND
KENT RD
ALDER ST
ST PATRICKS RD
DEVON ST
SHERLOCK ST
PATERSON RD
CALLINGTON ST
PHILIP ST
ST STEPHENS ST
MACKAY ST
SUFFOLK ST
CROSSWORD ST
LANSDOWNE ST

GOVAN MBEKI AVE
R102
FREDERICK ST
FORSTER ST
LESTER ST
VICTORIA QUAY

RICHMOND HILL
TULLA ST
Teachers Centre
DAGBREEK
HARTMAN ST
SMITH ST
CLARENDON CR
HUNT ST
KEMSLEY ST
CAMPBELL ST
DOLLERY ST
BELMONT TER

BAAKENS ST
Donkin Hill

WESTBOURNE OVAL
Technical College
RUSSELL RD
STANLEY ST
SOMERSET ST
MOFFAT ST
BAIN ST
RALEIGH ST
IRVINE ST
PARLIAMENT ST
ST
MUNICIPALITY
HAVELOCK ST
PEARSON ST
LAWRENCE RD
MILITARY RD

DONKIN RESERVE
Grand Gardens
Opera House
Library
Little Theatre
Edward
Feather Market Hall

Centrahil Horse Memorial
RINK ST
DONCASTER RD
ROBSON ST
CLYDE ST
WHITES RD
CASTLE HILL
PROSPECT HILL
COURT RD

Prince Alfred's Guard War Memorial
Park Drive Hospital
Great War Memorial
King George VI Art Gallery

ROSE ST
WESTERN RD
MUSEUM SQ
Trinity
BIRD ST
CUYLER ST
GORDON TER
FORT ST
ANNERLEY TER
TWICKENHAM ST
CUYLER ST

CENTRAL
ST. GEORGES PARK
ST GEORGE'S TENNIS CLUB
PARKRIDGE CR.
HALLACK ST
HOW AVE
NEWTON AVE
PARK DR.

HALLACK RD
WHITEHEAD AVE

St.Georges Hospital
**SETTLERS PARK
NATURE RESERVE**

Greenwood Primary
FORBES AVE
JUTLAND CR.
HUNTER AVE
SOMMERVILLE WAY
HARRIS RD
CUDMORE ST

BRICKMAKERS KLOOF
Fort Fredericks
ELLIS TER
PIER ST
SEYMOUR ST

SOUTH END

WALMER BLVD
KARMIN

Walmer Primary
VILLIERS RD
THIRD AVE
SECOND AVE
FIRST AVE

WALMER RD
GLADSTONE ST
DOUGLAS ST
UPPER VALLEY RD
BARNES ST
ANDERSON ST
BALFOUR ST
WYNDHAM ST
WYNDHAM LA.
WEBBER ST
PARTRIDGE DR.
BUTTERS AVE
HOY AVE
RANDALL ST
MITCHELL ST

M9
Victoria Park High
VICTORIA PARK
**VICTORIA PARK
OLD BOYS'
SPORTS GROUND**
**SOUTH END
CEMETERY**

FOURTH AVE
PLANE ST
CAITHNESS RD
ALBERT RD
UNION RD
ERNEST WALTER AVE
FIRST AVE

Victoria Park Grey Primary
Valley
ALLISTER MILLER DR.
M11

Walmer
Newton Park
Humansdorp/N2

Algoa Bay

Charl Malan
Quay

Port Elizabeth
Campanile

FLEMING ST

Airways
Terminal

GARDNER CIR.

M9

PIER ST

South End

MITCHELL ST

OAKWORTH RD

LAWHILL RD

INCHCAPE RD

NEWCON RD

SAYRE CR.

BRETON RD

LEA PL.

Humewood

HUMERAIL SPORTS
GROUND

FOREST HILL RD

"Apple Express"

1 NAMAQUA PL.
2 BOK ST

HUMEWOOD

Elizabeth
Donkin

CRANWELL DR.

CRANWELL CR.

CALDER CL.

CLOVER CR.

WOODHEAD DR.

HILTON CR.

Humewood Museum
Humewood Road

HUMEWOOD RD

GUTENIQUA PL.

POMMERN ST.

PERROT AVE

PASSAT ST

PAMIR ST

THEKLA CIR.

CHAPMAN AVE

Sea Breeze Express

Sea Cadet Base

HUMEWOOD EAST

Kings Beach Surf
Life Saving Club

WINDERMERE RD

DRIFTSANDS DR.

DUNDALK RD

KILLARNEY RD

CYPRUS AVE

Putt-Putt

Kings Beach

Conifer

OCEAN AVE

STRAND

HUMEWOOD

MANSIONS RD

BEACH RD

Humewood

MCARTHUR

GLENGARRY CR.

CHALMERS RD

ABERDOUR CR.

GLENGARRY CR.

KASWICH PL.

MARSHALL RD

NAPIER RD

SCHAFER

M11

CATHCART RD

AYLIFF ST

FERNDALE RD

SPRAI

VIEW AVE

HAPPY VALLEY DR.

Holiday Inn

Oceanarium

Port Elizabeth
Museum Complex

Caboose

City
Lodge

Skoemanskop

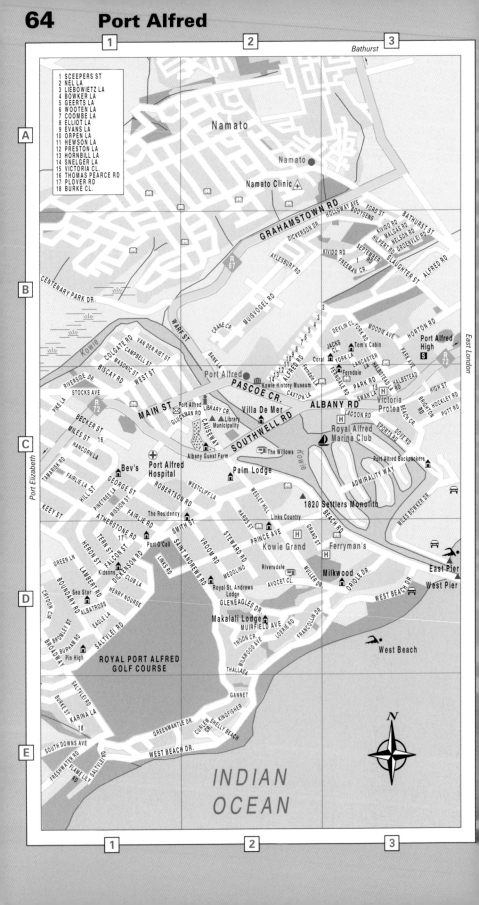

Bathurst

1. SCEEPERS ST
2. NEL LA
3. LIEBOWIETZ LA
4. BOWKER LA
5. GEERTS LA
6. WOOTEN LA
7. COOMBE LA
8. ELLIOT LA
9. EVANS LA
10. ORPEN LA
11. HEWSON LA
12. PRESTON LA
13. HORNBILL LA
14. SNELGER LA
15. VICTORIA CL.
16. THOMAS PEARCE RD
17. PLOVER RD
18. BURKE CL.

Namato

Namato

Namato Clinic

East London

Port Elizabeth

GRAHAMSTOWN RD

DICKERSON DR.

HOLLOWAY AVE

BOOYSENS

FORD ST

KIVIDO RD

BATHURST ST

MALGAS RD

NELSON RD

HILPERT RD

GROENVLEI RD

SLAUGHTER ST

ALFRED RD

SEPTEMBER

AYLESBURY RD

KIVIDO RD

FREEMAN CR.

CENTENARY PARK DR.

CRANE CR.

MUSVOGEL RD

DEVLIN CL.

YORK RD

MOODIE AVE

HORTON RD

Port Alfred High

WARE ST

JACKS CL.

Tom's Cabin

YORK LA

LANCASTER

PARK AVE

Kowie

COLGATE RD

VAN DER RIET ST

CAMPBELL ST

MASONIC ST

WEST ST

BANK LA

Coral

ALFRED RD

Ferndale

Ferndale

HALSTEAD RD

BISCAY RD

Port Alfred

Kowie History Museum

CAXTON LA

PARK RD

SWAN LA

HALBSTEAD RD

RIVERSIDE DR.

STOCKS AVE

PASCOE CR.

ALBANY RD

Victoria Protea

HIGH ST

PIKE LA

MAIN ST

Port Alfred

LIBRARY CR.

Villa De Mer

SOUTHWELL RD

LAGOON RD

SPORTS RD

BRIGHTON RD

HOCKLEY RD

PUTT RD

BECKER ST

GLUCKMAN RD

Library

Royal Alfred

DOVE CR.

MILES ST

HANCORN LA

CAUSEWAY

Municipality

Marina Club

BEACH CR.

Albany Guest Farm

The Willows

Kowie

Port Alfred Backpackers

TAMARISK RD

Bev's

Port Alfred

Palm Lodge

ADMIRALITY WAY

FAIRLIE LA

HILL ST

GEORGE ST

ROBERTSON RD

WESTCLIFF LA

KEEY ST

PINETREE LA

FAIRLIE RD

The Residency

MISSION ST

WESLEY HILL

Links Country

1820 Settlers Monolith

MILES BOWKER DR.

ATHERSTONE RD

SMITH ST

HARDS ST

PRINCE AVE

BEACH RD

TERN ST

Port O'Call

VROOM RD

STEWARD RD

Kowie Grand

GRAND ST

Ferryman's

East Pier

HERON ST

FALCON ST

SAINT ANDREWS RD

MEDOLINO

Riversdale

MULLER RD

Milkwood

ORIOLE DR.

West Pier

GREEN LN

Kidsons

DICKENSON

CLUB LA

Royal St. Andrews Lodge

AVOCET CL.

WEST BEACH DR.

LAMBERT RD

LINKS RD

HENRY NOURSE

GLENEAGLES DR.

FRANCOLIN DR.

Sea Star

Albatross

EAGLE LA

Makalali Lodge

MUIRFIELD AVE

BOUNDARY RD

BURHAM RD

SALTVLEI RD

LOERE RD

West Beach

BROADLAW

Pin High

MILKWOOD AVE

TROON CR.

BRAMLEY ST

ROYAL PORT ALFRED GOLF COURSE

THALLASA

CAVJON CIR.

SALTVLEI RD

GANNET

SALTVLEI RD

BURKE ST

KARINA LA

GREENMANTLE DR.

CURLEW

SHELLY BEACH

KINGFISHER

SOUTH DOWNS AVE

WEST BEACH DR.

FRESHWATER RD

FLAME LILY

R 67

R 72

R 72

INDIAN OCEAN

N

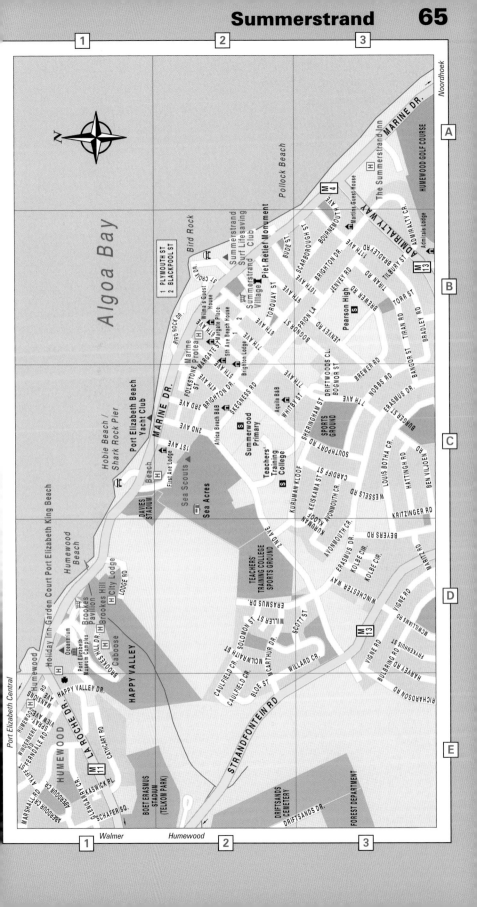

Noordhoek

MARINE DR.

HUMEWOOD GOLF COURSE

The Summerstrand Inn

H Martins Guest House

Admirals Lodge

ADMIRALTY WAY

M 4

M 13

BRADLEY BLVD

TILBURY ST

ADMIRALTY CR.

Pollock Beach

BURNEMOUTH AVE

11TH AVE

Summerstrand
Surf Lifesaving
Club

Bird Rock

ST CROIX DR.

PLYMOUTH ST
BLACKPOOL ST

BUDE ST

SCARBOROUGH ST

BRIGHTON DR.

TIRAN RD

Summerstrand
Village

Piet Retief Monument

TORQUAY ST

9TH AVE

10TH AVE

BOGNOR ST

JENVEY RD

BREWER RD

Pearson High S

TORR ST

BRADLEY RD

BANGOR ST

TIRAN ST

Wilma's Guest
House

Marine
Protea H

BIRD ROCK DR.

4TH AVE

MARGATE ST

5TH AVE Margate Place

Brighton Lodge

1 2

5th Ave Beach House

7TH AVE

8TH AVE

DRIFTWOODS CL.

BOGNOR ST

7TH AVE

NOBBS RD

ERASMUS DR.

BURGER ST

FOLKSTONE RD

3RD AVE

4TH AVE

BRIGHTON RD

SKEGNESS RD

Aquila B&B

WHITBY ST

SHERINGHAM ST

7TH AVE

SPORTS
GROUND

LOUIS BOTHA CR.

HATTINGH RD

BEN VILJOEN RD

Africa Beach B&B

Summerwood
Primary S

CARDIFF ST

SOUTHPORT RD

WESSELS RD

KRITZINGER RD

MARINE DR.

2ND AVE

1ST AVE

First Ave Lodge H

Beach

Sea Scouts

Sea Acres

Teachers'
Training
College S

KURUMAN KLOOF

KEISKAMA ST

AVONMOUTH CR.

BEYERS RD

Port Elizabeth Beach
Yacht Club

Hobie Beach /
Shark Rock Pier

DAVIES
STADIUM

AVONMOUTH CR.

ERASMUS DR.

KOLBE CIR.

KOLBE CIR.

VIGNE RD

Holiday Inn–Garden Court Port Elizabeth King Beach

Humewood
Beach

LODGE RD

Brookes
Pavilion

City Lodge H

H Brookes Hill

BROOKES HILL DR.

TEACHERS'
TRAINING COLLEGE
SPORTS GROUND

2ND AVE

ERASMUS DR.

WINCHESTER WAY

MARTI RD

VIGNE RD

MCWILLIAMS RD

FRAYENVALE ST

Oceanarium

Port Elizabeth
Museum Complex H

Caboose

H

MILLER ST

McARTHUR DR.

SCOTT ST

M 13

VIGNE RD

HARVEY RD

BULBRING RD

Port Elizabeth Central

Humewood H

SPRAY RD

VIEW AVE

HAPPY VALLEY

HAPPY VALLEY DR.

CAULFIELD CR.

McILWRAITH ST

SOLOMON ST

BLOE ST

CAULFIELD CR.

WILLARD CR.

STRANDFONTEIN RD

RICHARDSON RD

MANSION RD

HUMEWOOD RD

WINDERMERE RD

AYLIFF ST

FERNDALE RD

LA ROCHE DR.

HUMEWOOD

M 11

GLENGARRY CR.

KASWICK PL.

CATHCART RD

BOET ERASMUS
STADIUM
(TELKOM PARK)

SCHAFER SQ.

DRIFTSANDS
CEMETERY

FOREST DEPARTMENT

DRIFTSANDS DR.

MARSHALL RD

ABERDOUR CR.

ABERDOUR CR.

Walmer

Humewood

Algoa Bay

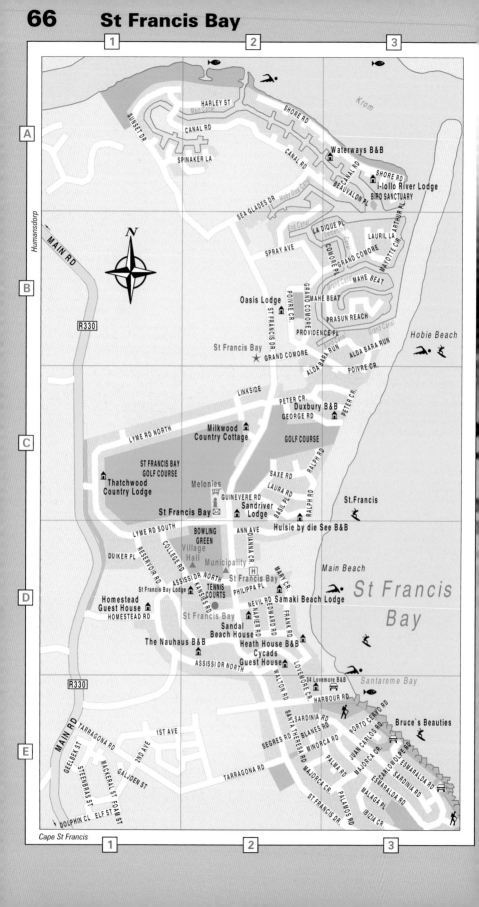

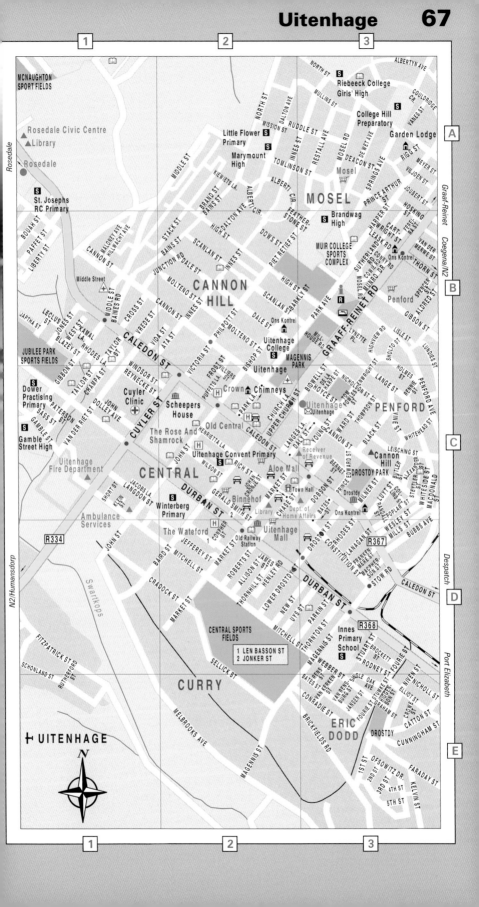

Karoo Heartland Karoo Heartla

The hot, dry and baking Karoo Heartland might seem unwelcoming at first glimpse (especially if that glimpse is of the aptly named Valley of Desolation!), but it has plenty to offer the sightseer and nature lover. Vast plains with plenty of wildlife to spot, majestic mountains, champagne air, as well as plenty of outdoor pursuits, including mountaineering and awesome paragliding. Graaff-Reinet is filled with history and charming architecture, while Cradock boasts the former house of author Olive Shreiner and Nieu-Bethesda is the location of the haunting Owl House.

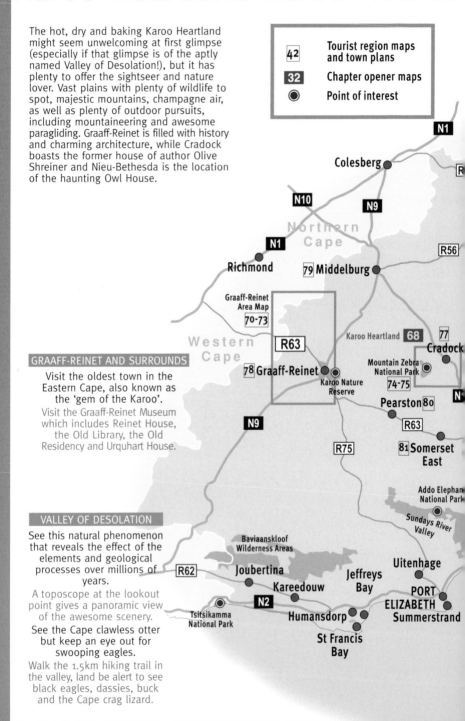

42	Tourist region maps and town plans
32	Chapter opener maps
◉	Point of interest

GRAAFF-REINET AND SURROUNDS

Visit the oldest town in the Eastern Cape, also known as the 'gem of the Karoo'.
Visit the Graaff-Reinet Museum which includes Reinet House, the Old Library, the Old Residency and Urquhart House.

VALLEY OF DESOLATION

See this natural phenomenon that reveals the effect of the elements and geological processes over millions of years.
A toposcope at the lookout point gives a panoramic view of the awesome scenery.
See the Cape clawless otter but keep an eye out for swooping eagles.
Walk the 1.5km hiking trail in the valley, land be alert to see black eagles, dassies, buck and the Cape crag lizard.

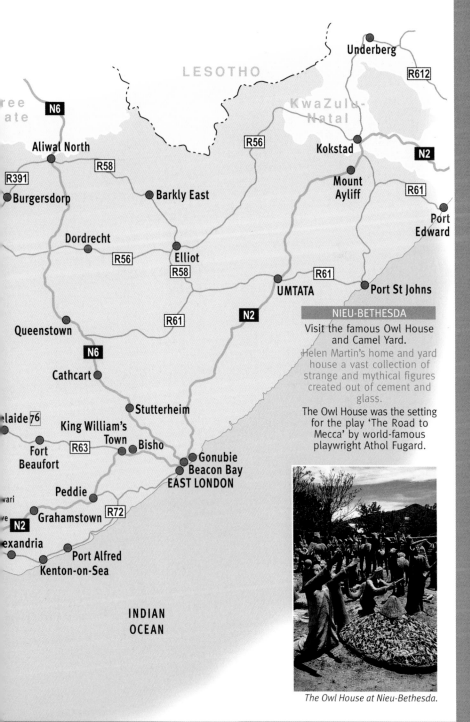

Underberg

R612

LESOTHO

KwaZulu-Natal

ree ate

N6

Aliwal North

R56

Kokstad

N2

R58

R391

Burgersdorp

Barkly East

Mount Ayliff

R61

Port Edward

Dordrecht

R56

Elliot

R58

R61

UMTATA

Port St Johns

Queenstown

R61

N2

NIEU-BETHESDA

Visit the famous Owl House and Camel Yard.

Helen Martin's home and yard house a vast collection of strange and mythical figures created out of cement and glass.

The Owl House was the setting for the play 'The Road to Mecca' by world-famous playwright Athol Fugard.

N6

Cathcart

Stutterheim

laide 76

King William's Town

Bisho

Fort Beaufort

R63

Gonubie
Beacon Bay
EAST LONDON

Peddie

wari

R72

N2

Grahamstown

exandria

Port Alfred
Kenton-on-Sea

INDIAN OCEAN

The Owl House at Nieu-Bethesda.

1 **2** **3**

24° 15'

Northern
Cape

Rooikop
2034m

A

Kranskop
2052m

44

Rheboksfontein

Kookfontein

31° 45'

Rhenosterfontein

Groot Hartbeesfontein

15

Waterkrans

1

Bloukrans

Enslin's Rus

B

Matjiesfontein
2068m

Groenvlei

19

25

Krugerskraal

Nooigedacht

Driefontein

Waterval

E a s t e r n

Mountain Lodge

Winterhoek

Tweefonteinspruit

C a p e

C

Stilfontein

Ou Tweefontein

Rondefontein

R388

Meltfontein

1416m

Murraysburg 32km

Oudeland

32° 00'

1879m

R
63

32

W e s t e r n

Damesfontein

Onrust

30

D

Poortjie

C a p e

8

Hoerkop
1906m

Boesmanskop
1677m

Grand View

Zuurplaats

29

R
63

E

Toorberg

Grassdale

Wolwekloof

Buffels

| 0 | 2 | 4 | 6 | 8km |

Scale 1 : 250 000

1 **72** **2** **3**

24° 15'

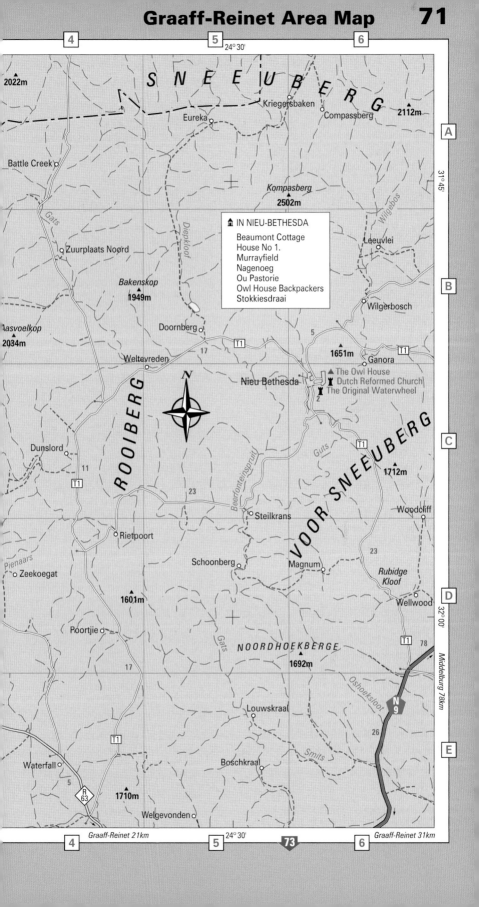

SNEEUBERG

2022m

Kriegersbaken

Eureka

Compassberg

2112m

Battle Creek

A

31° 45'

Kompasberg
2502m

Zuurplaats Noørd

Leeuvlei

Bakenskop
1949m

Wilgerbosch

B

asvoelkop
2034m

Doornberg

IN NIEU-BETHESDA

Beaumont Cottage
House No 1.
Murrayfield
Nagenoeg
Ou Pastorie
Owl House Backpackers
Stokkiesdraai

Weltevreden

17

T1

5

1651m

Ganora

T1

Nieu Bethesda

The Owl House
Dutch Reformed Church
The Original Waterwheel
2

ROOIBERG

N

Dunslord

11

T1

23

1712m

Woodcliff

C

VOOR SNEEUBERG

Steilkrans

Rietpoort

Pienaars

Zeekoegat

Schoonberg

Magnum

23

Rubidge Kloof

Wellwood

D

32° 00'

1601m

Poortjie

NOORDHOEKBERGE
1692m

T1

78

Middelburg 78km

17

Louwskraal

26

N9

T1

Waterfall

5

R63

1710m

Boschkraal

Smits

E

Welgevonden

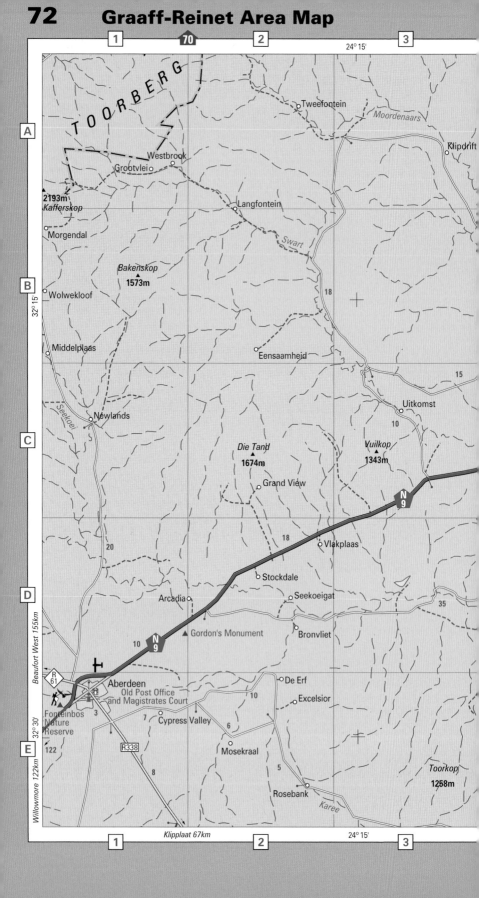

TOORBERG

Tweefontein

Moordenaars

Klipdrift

Westbrook

Grootvlei

2193m
Kafferskop

Langfontein

Swart

Morgendal

18

Bakenskop
1573m

Wolwekloof

Middelplaas

Eensaamheid

15

Seekoei

Newlands

Uitkomst

10

Die Tand
1674m

Vuilkop
1343m

Grand View

N9

20

18

Vlakplaas

Stockdale

Arcadia

Seekoeigat

35

▲ Gordon's Monument

Bronvliet

N9
10

De Erf

Aberdeen
**Old Post Office
and Magistrates Court**

Excelsior

R61

Fonteinbos
Nature
Reserve

3

7

Cypress Valley

10

6

122

R338

Mosekraal

Toorkop
1258m

5

8

Rosebank

Karee

Beaufort West 155km

Willowmore 122km

32° 15'

32° 30'

24° 15'

Klipplaat 67km

24° 15'

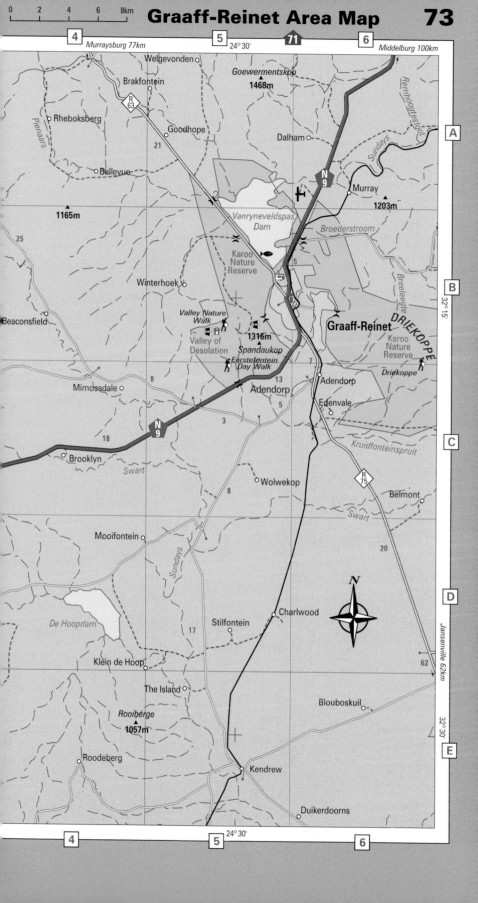

0   2   4   6   8km

4 Murraysburg 77km   **5** 24°30'   **71**   **6** Middelburg 100km

Welgevonden

Brakfontein

Goewermentskop
▲ 1468m

R 53

Rheboksberg

Goodhope

Dalham

A

Pienaars

21

Bellevue

N 9

Murray
▲ 1203m

▲ 1165m

25

Vanryneveldspas
Dam

Broederstroom

Sundays

Karoo
Nature
Reserve

Winterhoek

B 32°15'

Rembhoogtesloot

Beaconsfield

Valley Nature
Walk

Valley of
Desolation

▲ 1316m

Spandaukop

Graaff-Reinet

Karoo
Nature
Reserve

DRIEKOPPE

Breeleegte

Eerstefontein
Day Walk

Mimosadale

8

Adendorp

13

Adendorp

Driekoppe

7

N 9

3

5

Edenvale

18

Kruidfonteinspruit

Brooklyn

Swart

8

Wolwekop

R 75

Belmont

Swart

Mooifontein

20

De Hoopdam

N

Charlwood

D

17

Stilfontein

Jansenville 62km

Klein de Hoop

62

The Island

Rooiberge
▲ 1057m

Blouboskuil

32°30'

Roodeberg

E

Kendrew

Duikerdoorns

4   **5** 24°30'   **6**

1 Port Chalmers 9km   **2** 25° 30'   **3** Middelburg 94km

Rietfontein

9

R61

19

10

Rooileegte

N10

Salpeterkop
1515m

94

De Rust

6

R61

Wilgebooms

A

Doornhoek

**Mountain
Zebra
National
Park**

Morgenzon

B

14

Van Heerdenskraal

Kareebos

Ebenhaezer

Vaalkop
1401m

Nelskraal

Bossieskloof

C

Zebra-Park

21

Fleurviville

32° 15'

Weltevrede

R337

D

Bakenkop
1957m

*Swaershoek
Pass*

Brandhoek

Groothoek

G A N N A

Merino

E

Groenhoek

6

| 0 | 1 | 2 | 3 | 4km |

Scale 1 : 600 000

R337

8

Houtkloof

68

1 Pearston 68km   **2** 25° 30'   **3**

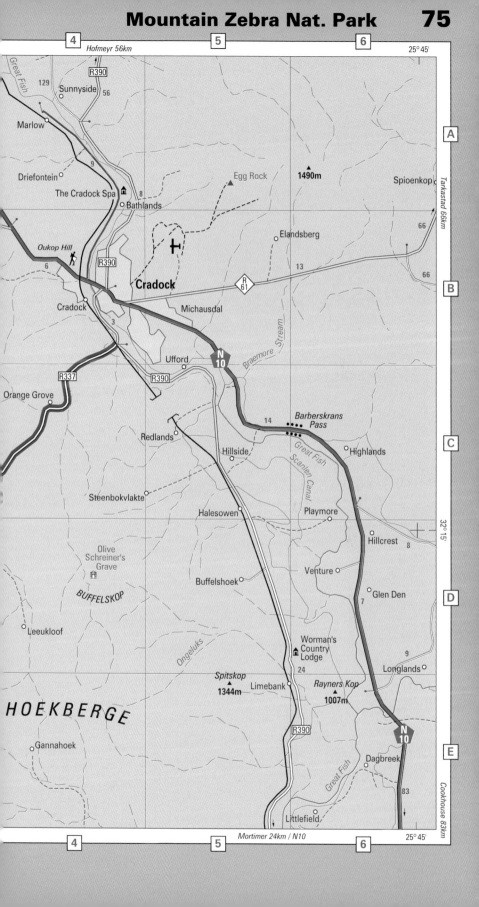

Great Fish

129

Sunnyside
56

R390

Marlow

A

9

Driefontein

Egg Rock
1490m

Spioenkop

Tarkastad 66km

The Cradock Spa
8

Bathlands

66

Oukop Hill

Elandsberg

R390

13

66

6

Cradock

R
61

B

Cradock

3

Michausdal

Braemore Stream

R337

Ufford

N
10

R390

Orange Grove

14

Barberskrans
Pass

Redlands

Great Fish

Highlands

C

Hillside

Scanlen Canal

32° 15'

Steenbokvlakte

Halesowen

Playmore

Hillcrest
8

Olive
Schreiner's
Grave

Venture

BUFFELSKOP

Buffelshoek

Glen Den

D

Leeukloof

7

9

Ongeluks

Worman's
Country
Lodge

Longlands

24

HOEKBERGE

Spitskop
1344m

Limebank

Rayners Kop
1007m

N
10

Gannahoek

R390

E

Great Fish

Dagbreek

Cookhouse 83km

83

Littlefield

25° 45'

Tarkastad

ASTER ST
DANIELS ST
PETER CROUCH ST
PERCY JOSEPH ST
DAWID KLAASEN ST
JAN DOUGLAS ST
WESSEL ROBERTS ST

R344

AIRFIELD

Adelaide
Primére S

ADAM FLEUR ST
ALFRED AURETS ST
GOLIOT MEIER ST
ALFRED MEYER ST

VILJOEN ST
MEINTJIE ST

ADELAIDE GOLF CLUB

619m

N

Furrow

MILL ST
DE WEY ST
LINK ST
POHL ST

R344

WINTERBURG AVE

PIET RETIEF AVE

Adelaide Hospital

Adelaide

Fort Beaufort

PLEIN ST
HADDON ST
VAN ST
GRAHAM ST
EIRIE ST

R63

THOMPSON ST
CHURCH ST
BUITEKANT ST
LEE ST
MARAIS ST

BON ACCORD ST
STRINGFELLOW
CONSTITUTION ST
MARGARET ST
GRAVE ST
QUEEN ST

Adelaide
Adelaide
Municipality
N.G.Kerk
POHL ST
THOMPSON ST
STOCKENSTROOM ST
RAUBENHEIMER ST
VAN WYK ST
WELSH ST
GREY ST
MARKET ST
Adelaide Century Lodge
Heritage Museum

UPTON ST

QUEEN ST

SMITH ST
CHURCH ST

Koonap

PRINCESS ST

R63

Cowie

Bedford

0   200   400   600m
Scale 1 : 20 000

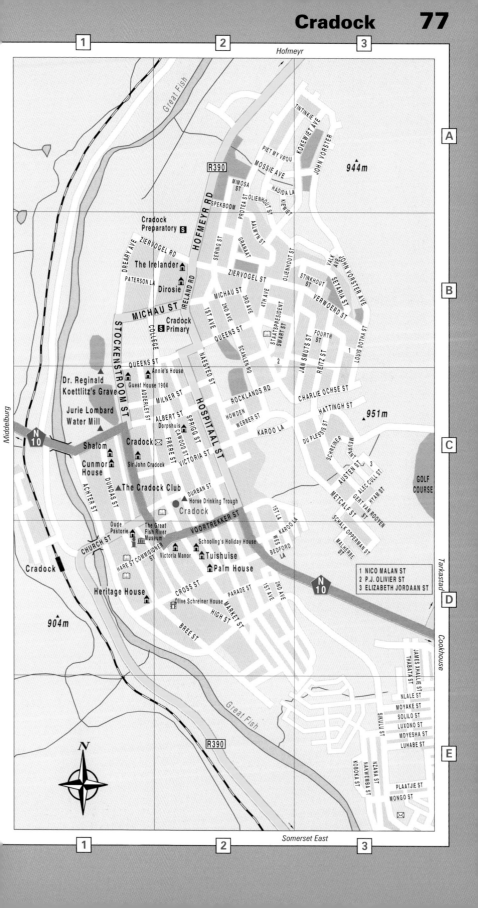

Hofmeyr

1 2 3

Great Fish

A

Tintinkie Ave

Kokewiet Ave

John Vorster

Piet My Vrou

Mossie Ave

944m

R390

Mimosa St

Spekboom

Hadida La

Olienhout St

Protea St

Kiewiet

HOFMEYR RD

Sering St

Granaat

Aalwyn St

Valk Ave

John Vorster Ave

Cradock
Preparatory

Ziervogel Rd

Drear y Ave

The Irelander

Paterson La

Ziervogel St

Michau St

O 1ienhout St

Stinkhout St

Setaria St

Verwoerd St

Louis Botha St

B

Dirosie

IRELAND RD

MICHAU ST

1st Ave

2nd Ave

3rd Ave

4th Ave

Staatspresident
Swart St

Fourth St

COLLEGE

Cradock
Primary

Queens St

Scanlen Rd

Jan Smuts St

Reitz St

1

2

STOCKENSTROOM ST

Queens St

Annie's House

Guest House 1904

Adderley St

Milner St

NAESTED ST

HOSPITAAL ST

Rocklands Rd

Howden

Webber St

Karoo La

Charlie Ochse St

Hattingh St

951m

Dr. Reginald
Koettlitz's Grave

Jurie Lombard
Water Mill

N10

Shalom

Cunmor
House

Dundas St

Achter St

Albert St

Dorpshuis

Sprigg St

Canwood St

Frere St

Victoria St

Cradock

Sir John Cradock

The Cradock Club

Cradock

Durban St

Horse Drinking Trough

Du Plessis St

Schreiner

Meurant

Austen St

Geyr van Rooyen

Hyam St

Alec Cull St

Metcalf St

C

GOLF
COURSE

Oude
Pastorie

The Great
Fish River
Museum

Church St

Hare St

Commisioner St

Victoria Manor

Schooling's Holiday House

Voortrekker St

Tuishuise

Palm House

1st La

Wes

Bedford
La

Karoo La

Schalk Opperman St

Malherbe St

Cradock

Heritage House

Cross St

Olive Schreiner House

Parade St

Market St

High St

2nd Ave

1st Ave

N10

1 NICO MALAN ST
2 P.J. OLIVIER ST
3 ELIZABETH JORDAAN ST

D

904m

Bree St

Great Fish

R390

James Xhallie St

Thabata St

Nlale St

Moyake St

Solilo St

Luxono St

Mdyesha St

Luhabe St

Sikulu St

Nzana St

Nxwenba St

Koboka St

Plaatjie St

Mongo St

E

N

Middelburg

Cradock

Tarkastad

Cookhouse

1 2 3

Somerset East

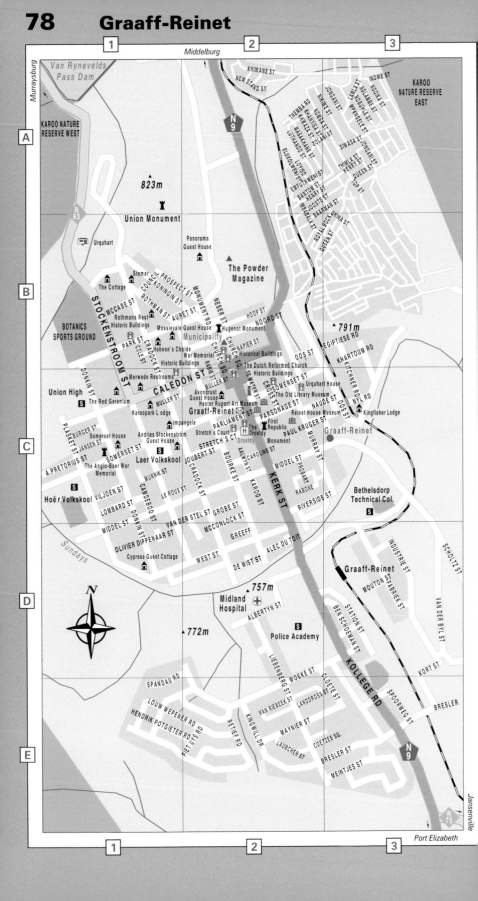

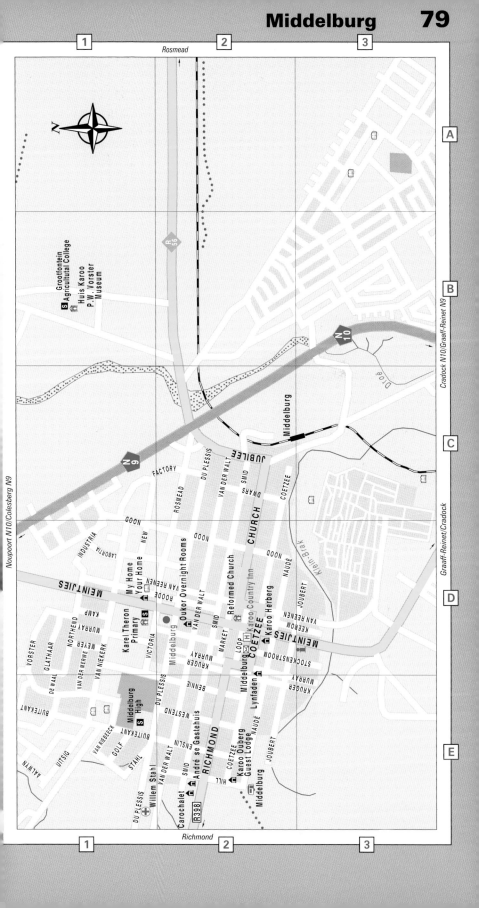

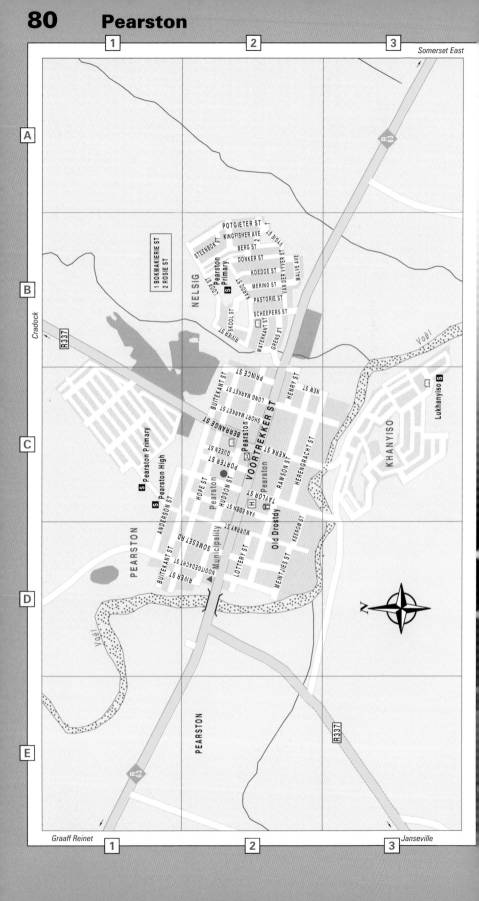

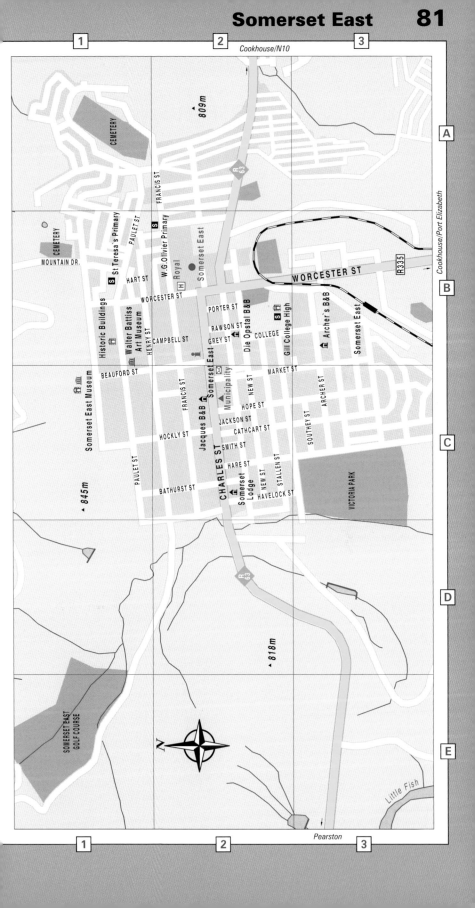

Amatola Mountains Amatola M

The Amatola Mountains are shrouded in mystery ... yet at the same time they offer spectacular scenery! Nature-lovers will feel they have come home when they spend time in this region, and its quaint towns and villages are steeped in the history of Xhosa culture, the struggle for liberation, as well as the trials and tribulations of the early settlers who brought with them everything the western world has to offer (good and bad!). Outdoor enthusiasts will thrive on the mountainbiking, hiking, rock climbing, kayaking and flyfishing for trout that is on offer here, while Lord of the Rings devotees will delight in knowing that 'their author' (JRR Tolkein) found his inspiration to write The Hobbit in the charming town of Hogsback, with its distinct English character and thickly-forested surrounds.

42	Tourist region maps and town plans
32	Chapter opener maps
◉	Point of interest

N1

Colesberg

N10   N9

N1

Northern Cape

R56

Richmond

Middelburg

KING WILLIAM'S TOWN AND SURROUNDS

Visit the Steve Biko Garden of Remembrance where the activist is buried.

Enrich yourself culturally by visiting the many historical buildings.

See the site of the Bisho Massacre outside the Bisho Stadium between Bisho and King William's Town.

The Old Military Reserve boasts a cannon presented to the town by Major General Earley-Wilmot.

Western Cape

R63

Graaff-Reinet

Karoo Nature Reserve

Mountain Zebra National Park

Cradoc

N9

Pearston

R63

R75

Somerset East

Addo Eleph National Pa

Sundays River Valley

HIKING IN THE AMATOLA MOUNTAINS

The Amatola Hiking Trail starts 23km from King William's Town and ends 3km away from Hogsback. The trail offers great scenery, cool conditions in hot weather and numerous amphibian-rich rock pools and waterfalls.

The Stutterheim and Kologha Hiking Trails is 35km long and should take two days, leading you through a yellowwood forest and past a number of waterfalls. The endpoint of the hike is at the Kologha Forest Station.

Baviaanskloof Wilderness Areas

R62   Joubertina

Kareedouw

N2

Tsitsikamma National Park

Humansdorp

St Francis Bay

Jeffreys Bay

Uitenhage

PORT ELIZABETH

Summerstran

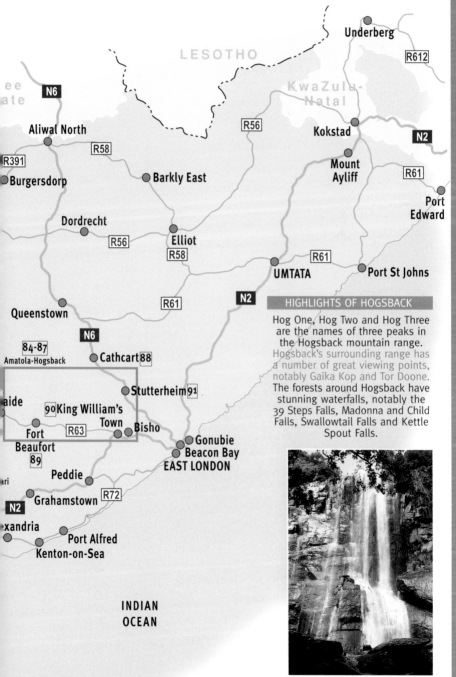

LESOTHO

KwaZulu-Natal

Underberg

R612

N6

Aliwal North

R56

Kokstad

N2

ee ate

R391

R58

Burgersdorp

Barkly East

Mount Ayliff

R61

Port Edward

Dordrecht

R56

Elliot

R58

R61

UMTATA

Port St Johns

Queenstown

R61

N2

N6

84-87
Amatola-Hogsback

Cathcart 88

Stutterheim 91

aide

90 King William's Town

Bisho

Fort Beaufort
89

R63

Gonubie
Beacon Bay
EAST LONDON

ari

Peddie

N2

Grahamstown

R72

xandria

Port Alfred
Kenton-on-Sea

INDIAN
OCEAN

HIGHLIGHTS OF HOGSBACK

Hog One, Hog Two and Hog Three are the names of three peaks in the Hogsback mountain range. Hogsback's surrounding range has a number of great viewing points, notably Gaika Kop and Tor Doone. The forests around Hogsback have stunning waterfalls, notably the 39 Steps Falls, Madonna and Child Falls, Swallowtail Falls and Kettle Spout Falls.

Madonna and Child Falls, Hogsback.

Tarkastad 61km

1   **2**   26° 30'   **3**

Adelaide 100km

R344

Winterberg

9

22

Groenkop

Site of Siege of
Hartebeesfontein
8th Frontier War

17

Waylands Farm

Koonap

Hikes to Rock
Art Sites

A

32° 30'

Suiwerfontein

Post Retief

DIDIM

11

Piet Retief
House Site

KLEIN-
WINTERBERG

12

12

Katberg State
Forest

B

Koonap

Fort Fordyce
Boshoek
Outspan

5

Travellers
Rest

Mpofu Hut

Mpofu

Ntlohi
Lodge

7

Mpofu Lodge

Mpofu
Nature Reserve

Kaalhoek

Iimbabala Lodge

C

Koedoeskloof
Game Farm

Pakamisa
House

Lourie
Rest House

9

Harris Hut

*Fullers
Hoek Pass*

Fort Fordyce
State Forest

Blinkwater

Adelaide 3km

3

Endwell Farm

12

Water
Mill

D

32° 45'

18

R63

Kroomie

R67

19

Fort Beaufort

Xuxuwa

16

R63

LIkley

5

R344

7

R67

| IN FORT BEAUFORT |
| Pete's Accommodation |
| Traveller's Lodge |

E

Koonap

10

The Tower
581m

17

10

| 0 | 2 | 4 | 6 | 8km |

Scale 1 : 250 000

R 67

Glenfinlas
Guest Cottage

E L A N D S B E R G

A

32°30'

Cathcart 47km

Katberg
Pass

Katberg State
Forest

H

Katberg
Protea Hotel

6

Nico Malan Pass

9

Seymour

Elands

Balfour

Anglican
Church

Fort Armstrong

9

Sundial

Kat River
Dam

16

Michels
Pass

B

Hogsback Arminel
Mountain Lodge

5

17

Lushington

Beckley's Cottages

H

Hyde Park Chalets

H

Kings Lodge Hotel

**Hogsback
Pass**

86

5

R 67

12

24

21

Hogsback

J U A N A S B E R G

10

Pefferskop
Pass

1085m
Pefferskop

KwaKyaletu

R345

i

War Memorial
1850

C

KwaMpundo

7

5

Tyumerivier
Dam

19

Melani

Majwareni

KwaMlalandle

Rwarwe

32°45'

King William's Town 62km

8

KwaNgwevu

KwaNgobe

KwaNkobonkobo

10

D

Martello
Tower

Fort Beaufort Museum

eRhoxeni

Lovedale
Mission

Ncera

Savoy

9

eSigingqini

KwaMavuso

De Beers Centenary
Fort Hare
University

R345

Tyutyuza

Victoria
Bridge

Mdala

Kwezana

4

5

Mtombo

Gudwini

R 63

eMxhelo

Alice

Igudu

Kat

8

5

eDrayini

Red
Hill

14

Ngwenya

Tower Cuttings

3

2

E

KwaSityi

R345

Tyume

Bhulurha

KwaCapo

1 27° 00' **2** Cathcart 30km **3**

A

32° 30'

N

ELANDSBERG

R345

Tweedale Farm

33

Gaika's Kop
1963m

B

H   O   L   E

Tor Doone
1565m

Amatola Hiking Trail

Cata

Kwa Nyanga

Beckley's
Cottages
Hyde Park
Chalets
Hogsback Arminel
Mountain Lodge
Amatola
Ngobazana

Cata Dam

19

85 Hogsback
Pass
Kings
Lodge
Hotel
Hogsback Mt. Cabins

THE HOGSBACK

21

Hogsback

KwaKyaletu

A
M
A
T
O
L
A

Wolf River
Forest

Wolf

Gxulu

Keiskammahoek

Fort Eyre   H

C War Memorial
850

R345

KwaNomadolo

KwaMpundo

Alice 20km

32° 45'

Keiskammahoek

Gwiligwil

Tyumerivier
Dam

Amatole
Basin

Sandile
Dam

Red Hill Pass

Upper
Ngqumeya

Majwareni

Keiskamma

Keiskamma

Rwarwe

Ncera

Gaika's
Grave

28

20

D

Zanyokwe

R352

Tyutyuza

Burnshill

Alice 19km

Mtombo
Gudwini
KwaMfiki

Grave of
Kama

Rabe

Dimbaza

Red
Hill
Igudu
14

Gowena

R63

Ngcamngeni

3

Debe Nek

Dimbaza

Ngwenya

Middledrift

15

E

KwaSityi

eXesi

Keiskamma

Qanda

Willmerton

Zihlahleni

Debe

KwaCapo

Newtown

Maipase

1 27° 00' **2** **3**

7

Toise
Backpackers
Lodge

Ndumangeni

N6

Toise

eNgqande

21

2

A

32° 30'

Fort Cunynghame
State Forest

Fort
Cunynghame

Little Thomas

Bagatelle

15

Dohne
Fortified
Ganger's
Cottage

H

R352

X O L O R A

Kologha Forest

Kologha
Hiking
Trails

Kologha

Kologha Park

Manderson County
House

8

Croft Guest
Cottage

H

Lavender
Lodge

The Weir
B&B

Bethal Mission

B

4

Mlungisi

Kubusi

3

Stutterheim

1617m
Mt. Thomas

Kubusi
State Forest

Gubu

Kubusi

Wriggleswade
Dam

9

R352

5

Gubu
Caravan
Park

Gubu
Dam

14

Waterfall
Farm

6

Gasela

9

N6

Dontsa
Pass

Sandile's
Grave 1878

Dontsa
Forest

8

3

2

7

6

Amabele

C

67km East London 68km

Keiskamma

1420m
Mt. Kemp

6

R
63

14

4

6

Frankfort

Southdown

D

32° 45'

Amatola Hiking Trail

Maden
Dam

KwaMxhanga

3

4

9

KwaGana

Nkqonkweni

Peelton

8

Rooikrans Dam

14

4

R346

Tyusha

KwaMangati

9

5

Braunschweig

Sixekweni

5

Twezana

Rhamnyiba

14

5

4

Buffalo

12

Merino Vale

E

KwaDikidikana

KwaMdingi

14

Ngqingeni

R
63

Pirie

23

King William's
Town

Bisho

Kings
Cross

8

Mzantsi

Liefeldt

Amathole

Plumbago

Yellowwoods

Blaney

Bulembu

KwaLenza

British Kaffrarian
Savings Bank

Crown

H

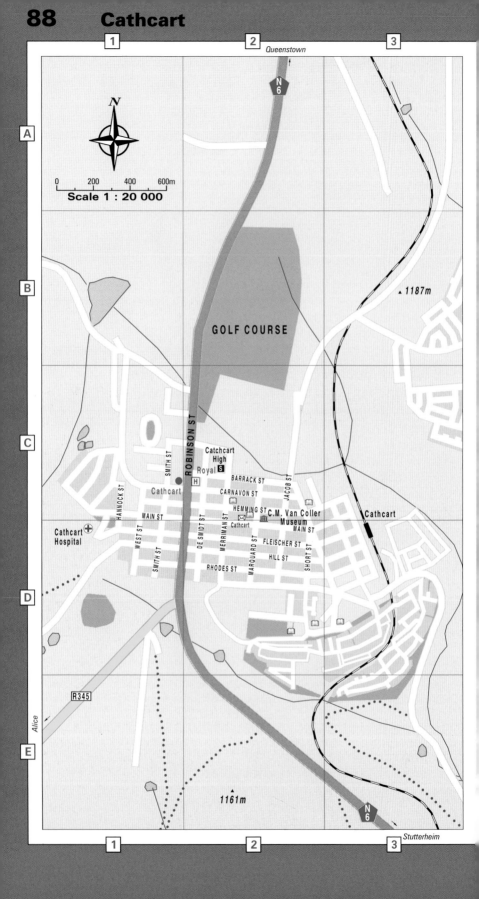

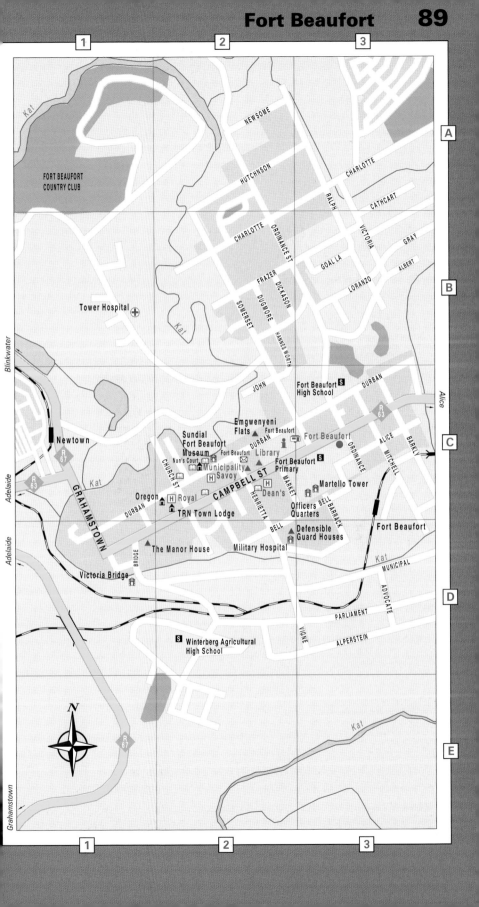

FORT BEAUFORT
COUNTRY CLUB

Tower Hospital

Newtown

Fort Beaufort
High School

Emgwenyeni
Flats

Sundial
Fort Beaufort
Museum

Nun's Court

Municipality

Savoy

Oregon

Royal

TRN Town Lodge

Dean's

Fort Beaufort

Library

Fort Beaufort
Primary

Martello Tower

Officers Bell
Quarters

Defensible
Guard Houses

The Manor House

Military Hospital

Fort Beaufort

Victoria Bridge

Winterberg Agricultural
High School

CAMPBELL ST

GRAHAMSTOWN

Blinkwater

Adelaide

Adelaide

Grahamstown

Alice

Kat

Stutterheim   KwaMangati

A

B

C

D

E

1   2   3

Grahamstown

Komga

East London

Kidd's Beach

West

Albatross Ave

Kingfisher

Turbine Rd

Peters

Hood St

Oak

R346

Reserve Rd

King William's Town

Old Powder Magazine

The Presidency

SA Missionary Museum

Berkeley St

Percy St

Mary St

Smith St

Cross Bank

Old Methodist Manse

Wellington

Bridge

Botanic

Garden

Walker

Maclean St

The Town Hall

Alexandra Rd

Beatrice

Fleet

Catherine

Chapel St

Amatola Rd

Kama St

Durban St

Edward St

Market St

Weir

King William's Town

Albert Rd

King Rd

Dale College Boys' Primary

Amathole Museum

Queens Rd

Herena

Whittaker

Dyer

New St

Pottinger

Burton

Amatola Rd

Durban St

New St

Bryson

Nowers St

Raglan St

Chamberlain

Gerhardi

Dale College

Queens Rd

Marais Rd

Alamein Cr.

Piet Retief Ave

Dan Pienaar Ave

Nico Malan Dr.

Van der Zee Cr.

Alamein Cr.

Burton

R63

Kaffrarian High

Grey Hospital

Grosvenor

British Kaffrarian Savings Bank

Municipality

King William's Town

Taylor St

Cathcart St

Botanical Gardens and Nature Reserve

Ayliff St

Arthur St

Buffalo Rd

Eales St

Napier St

Cambridge Rd

Leopold St

Lower Mount St

Hoёrskool de Vos Malan

Beaumont Rd

Upper Mount St

Lonsdale St

Gordon St

Innes St

Maitland Rd

McIntyre Rd

King Rd

Freee St

The Cottage

Hemmingways Guest & Conference

Reflections B&B

Dreamer's Guest House

Cemetery

Woodhouse St

Symons Ave

Douglas St

Central Primary

Victoria

Iqonce Secondary

King William's Town

Grey St

Louisa St

Thomas St

Alice St

Woodhouse St

Crown

Buffalo Rd

Henry St

Douglas St

Cambridge Rd

Lydia

Wynyark

Paul

Buffalo Rd

Fleming

N2

R346

Hargreaves Ave

Buffalo

N

House of Steven Biko

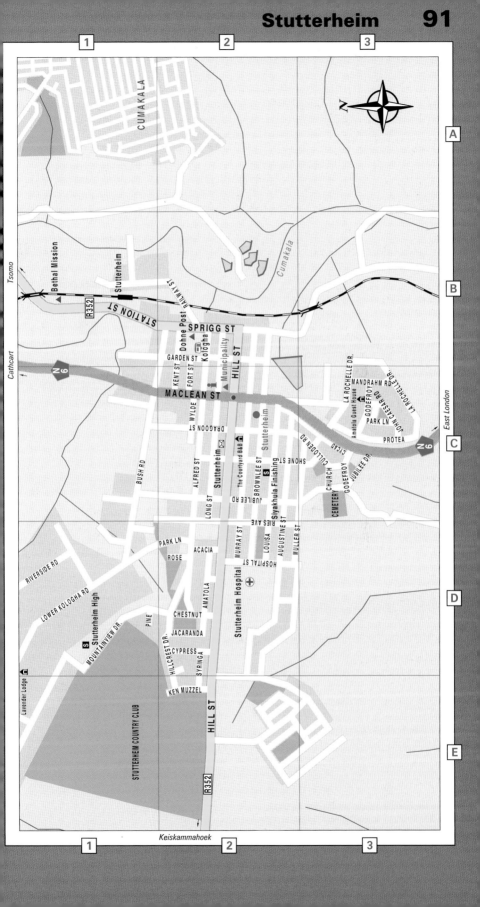

Friendly N6 Friendly N6 Friendly

The N6 is a direct link from Bloemfontein in the Free State to East London, along a charming route that befits its title of Friendly: hospitality, activities and magnificent scenery abound! Ben MacDhui has ski slopes to test the success of your European holidays, there are trout-packed cold streams (dress warm!), thick and lush forests, Bushman cave art to admire, as well as farms and farmers to welcome you into their easy way of life (or so city slickers might presume). The route will put you in touch with some historic towns such as Barkly East, Rhodes, Lady Grey, Elliot, Aliwal North, Burgersdorp and Queenstown.

42	Tourist region maps and town plans
32	Chapter opener maps
◉	Point of interest

QUEENSTOWN

Named after Queen Victoria, Queenstown is the largest town throughout the Cape Midlands.

Queenstown's bounteous display of roses is the toast of the town.

Town planners created Queenstown around a hexagonal centre. They reasoned that it would be easier to defend the town from the central square.

The early settlers and brave fighters in the Frontier Wars are remembered in the town's Frontier Museum and the Queenstown Collectors' museum.

FRIENDLY TOWNS WITH A PAST

Rhodes, named after the famous Cecil John Rhodes, is a popular retreat for artists.

Lady Grey's Footsteps into the Past trail leads you around the town's historic hotspots.

Elliot is close to South Africa's longest San rock art collection, found on the Denorbin Farm.

Aliwal North has popular hot springs and the Garden of Remembrance (honouring victims of the Anglo-Boer War).

Burgersdorp is filled with history, from the old town jail, to Stormberg battlesite, the Cultural History Museum and even an Afrikaans Language Monument.

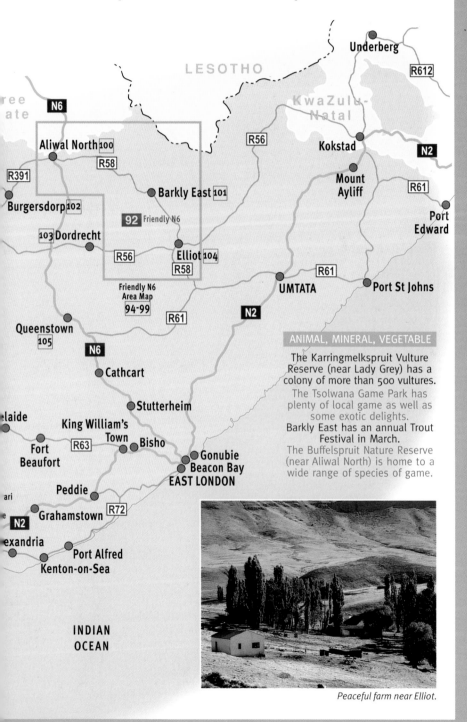

Underberg

R612

LESOTHO

KwaZulu-Natal

N6

R56

Aliwal North 100

Kokstad

N2

R58

Mount Ayliff

R391

R61

Burgersdorp 102

Barkly East 101

Port Edward

92 Friendly N6

103 Dordrecht

R56

Elliot 104

R61

R58

UMTATA

Port St Johns

Friendly N6 Area Map

94-99

R61

N2

Queenstown 105

N6

ANIMAL, MINERAL, VEGETABLE

The Karringmelkspruit Vulture Reserve (near Lady Grey) has a colony of more than 500 vultures.

Cathcart

The Tsolwana Game Park has plenty of local game as well as some exotic delights.

Stutterheim

Barkly East has an annual Trout Festival in March.

laide

King William's Town

Bisho

The Buffelspruit Nature Reserve (near Aliwal North) is home to a wide range of species of game.

Fort Beaufort

R63

Peddie

Gonubie

Beacon Bay

EAST LONDON

ari

Grahamstown

N2

R72

exandria

Port Alfred

Kenton-on-Sea

INDIAN OCEAN

Peaceful farm near Elliot.

Klipplaatsfontein
Swartfontein
Ventersrust

26° 45'
Rouxville 12km

N6
12

30° 30'
Zeekoegat
1561m
Klipfontein
Kalwerhok
Gedagtenis
Soetvlei

A
Strydpoort Dam
Weltevreden

Zuurplaat
23
19
Grootdam

Goedemoed 15km
15
1644m
Goede Frauw
Beestekraalnek
Anglo Boer War Monument

Free State
Brughalte
Denmark
14

Marieta
Rock Art Sterkstroom Farm

B
17
Quits
Wanganella
6
1551m

Burgersdorp 42km
Orange
Dukathole
Buffelspruit Nature Reserve
Oorlogsfontein
Lusthof
Mooifontein

Masango
R58
2
5
Aliwal North
Buffelsbaden
19
Kraai

C
Gryskoppan
42
16

30° 45'
N6
9

KRAMBERG
Maletswai
Maynier
Pollie
Braamkop
1503m
Braamspruit

Krambergspruit
Melkspruit
Kraaibrug

Oliewenfontein
Rock Art Kalkoenkrans
Element
12

1857m
24
1659m
Mount Carmel

D
Spes Bona
Klipspruit
Lagerfontein
Loskop

Krompoort
1605m

0 2 4 6 8 10km
Scale 1 : 300 000

1899m
Ruigtevlei
N6
10
Rietvlei

Oliviersspruit
Vineyard

Ezelshoek
9
Dwarsvlei

E
Stormberg
2099m
Croxteth
37

Hillside
Rock Art
Geluksoord
Eldorado
Windvogelspruit

Dwaalfontein
Watervlei
1731m

26° 45'
Jamestown 37km

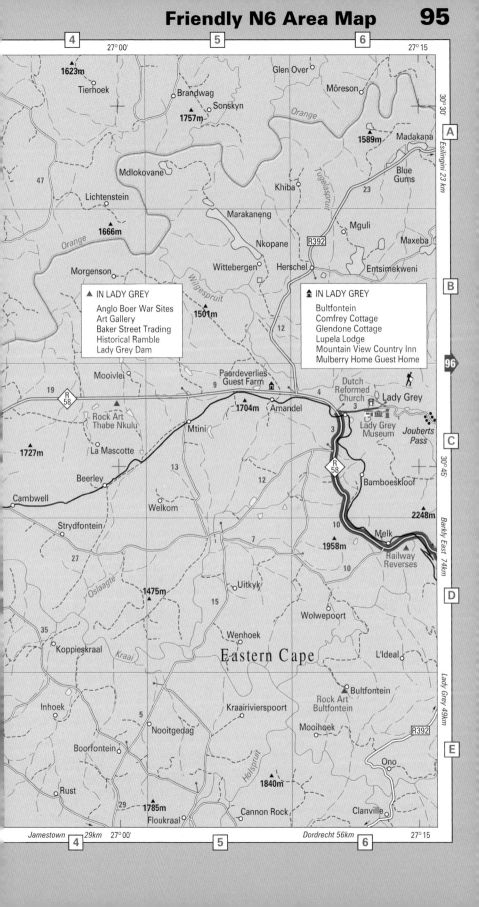

IN LADY GREY

- Anglo Boer War Sites
- Art Gallery
- Baker Street Trading
- Historical Ramble
- Lady Grey Dam

IN LADY GREY

- Bultfontein
- Comfrey Cottage
- Glendone Cottage
- Lupela Lodge
- Mountain View Country Inn
- Mulberry Home Guest Home

Eastern Cape

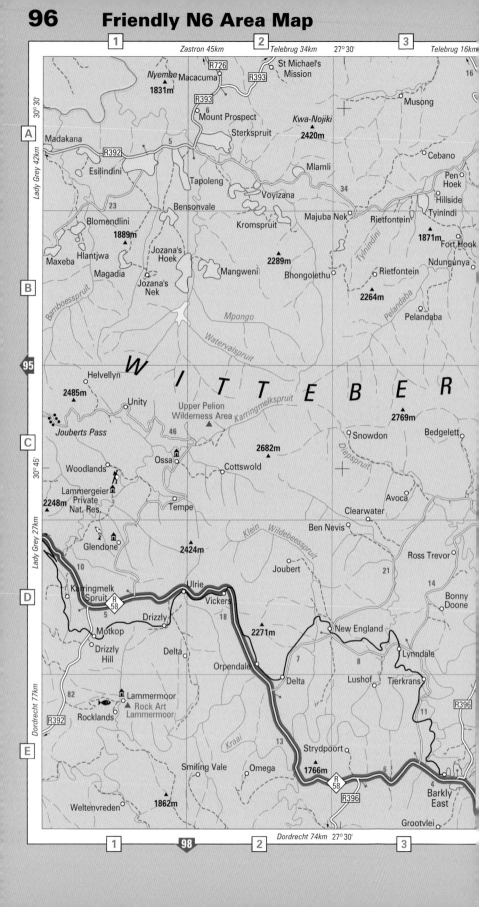

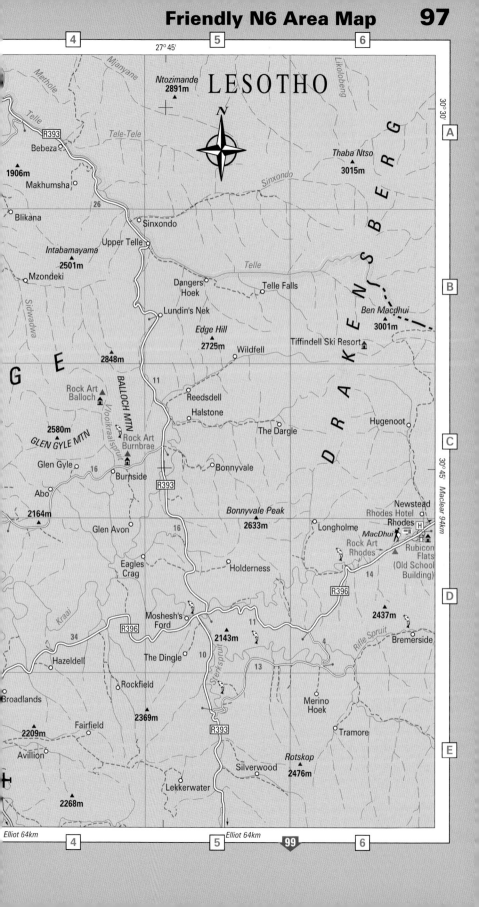

27° 45'

Methole

Mjanyane

Likoloebeng

Telle

R393

Bebeza

1906m

Makhumsha

Tele-Tele

Ntozimande
2891m

LESOTHO

N

Sinxondo

Thaba Ntso
3015m

30° 30'

A

Blikana

Intabamayama
2501m

Mzondeki

26

Sinxondo

Upper Telle

Telle

Dangers
Hoek

Telle Falls

D
R
A
K
E
N
S
B
E
R
G

B

Sidwadwa

G
E

2848m

Lundin's Nek

Edge Hill
2725m

Wildfell

Tiffindell Ski Resort

Ben Macdhui
3001m

Rock Art
Balloch

BALLOCH MTN

11

Reedsdell

Halstone

The Dargle

Hugenoot

30° 45' Maclear 94km

C

2580m
GLEN GYLE MTN

Glen Gyle

Abo

16

Vlooikraalspruit

Rock Art
Burnbrae

Burnside

R393

Bonnyvale

2164m

Glen Avon

16

Bonnyvale Peak
2633m

Longholme

Rock Art
Rhodes

Newstead
Rhodes Hotel
Rhodes
MacDhui

Rubicon
Flats
(Old School
Building)

H

D

Eagles
Crag

Holderness

14

2437m

Bremerside

Kraai

34

R396

Moshesh's
Ford

R396

The Dingle

2143m

10

Sterkspruit

11

13

4

Rifle Spruit

Hazeldell

Rockfield

Broadlands

Fairfield

2209m

Avillion

2369m

R393

Merino
Hoek

Tramore

E

Lekkerwater

Silverwood

Rotskop
2476m

2268m

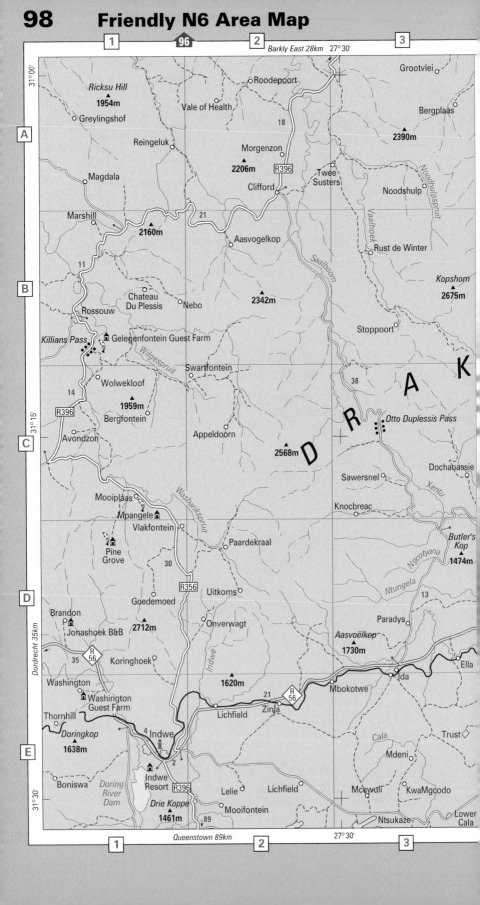

1   96   **2**   Barkly East 28km   27° 30'   **3**

31° 00'

Ricksu Hill
1954m

Greylingshof

Roodepoort

Grootvlei

Vale of Health

Bergplaas

2390m

Reingeluk

Morgenzon

18

A

Magdala

2206m   R396

Clifford

Twee
Susters

Noodshulp

Marshill

21

2160m

Aasvogelkop

Rust de Winter

Kopshorn
2675m

11

B

Chateau
Du Plessis

Nebo

2342m

Stoppoort

Rossouw

Killians Pass

Gelegenfontein Guest Farm

Swartfontein

38

D R A K

Wolwekloof

14

R396

1959m

Bergfontein

Appeldoorn

Otto Duplessis Pass

C

Avondzon

2568m

Dochanassie

31° 15'

Sawersnel

Knocbreac

Mooiplaas

Mpangele

Vlakfontein

Paardekraal

*Butler's
Kop*
1474m

Pine
Grove

30

R356

Uitkoms

13

D

Goedemoed

Onverwagt

Paradys

Brandon

Jonashoek B&B

2712m

Aasvoëlkop
1730m

R
56   35

Koringhoek

Ella

Washington

1620m

R
56

Mbokotwe

Ida

Washington
Guest Farm

21

Zinja

Thornhill

Lichfield

Cala

Trust

Doringkop
1638m

4   Indwe

Mdeni

E

Boniswa

*Doring
River
Dam*

2

Indwe
Resort   R396

Lelie

Lichfield

Mcewuli

KwaMgcodo

Drie Koppe
1461m

89

Mooifontein

Ntsukaze

Lower
Cala

31° 30'

Dordrecht 35km

1   Queenstown 89km   **2**   27° 30'   **3**

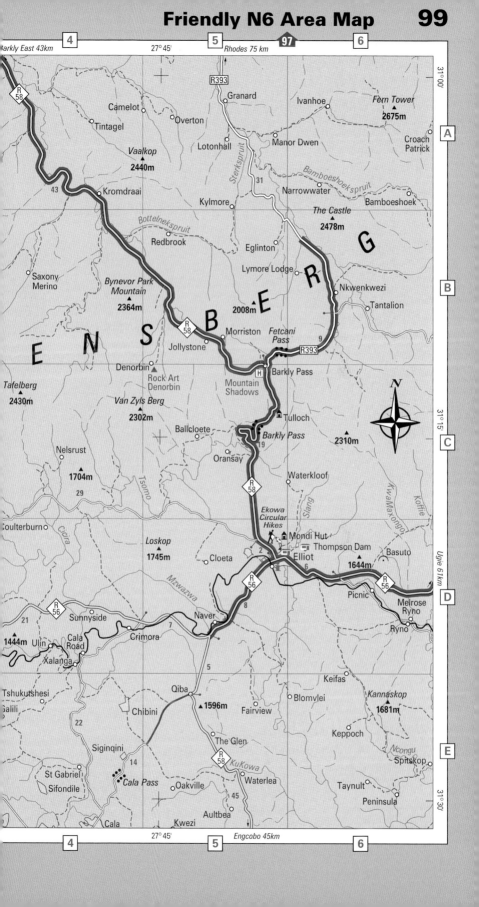

R393

Granard

Ivanhoe

Fern Tower
▲ **2675m**

Camelot

Overton

Manor Dwen

Croach
Patrick

Tintagel

Lotonhall

Vaalkop
▲ **2440m**

Sterkspruit

Bamboeshoekspruit

31

43

Kromdraai

Kylmore

Narrowwater

Bamboeshoek

Bottelneksspruit

The Castle
▲ **2478m**

Saxony
Merino

Redbrook

Eglinton

Lymore Lodge

Nkwenkwezi

*Bynevor Park
Mountain*
▲ **2364m**

2008m ▲

Tantalion

R58

Morriston

*Fetcani
Pass*

9

Jollystone

R393

Denorbin

*Rock Art
Denorbin*

H

Barkly Pass

*Mountain
Shadows*

Tafelberg
▲ **2430m**

Van Zyls Berg
▲ **2302m**

Ballcloete

Tulloch

Barkly Pass

▲ **2310m**

Nelsrust
▲ **1704m**

Oransay

19

29

Waterkloof

R58

Tsomo

Slang

Kwa Maxongo

Koffie

Coulterburn

*Ekowa
Circular
Hikes*

Loskop
▲ **1745m**

Cloeta

2

Mondi Hut

Thompson Dam

Basuto

Elliot

6

▲ **1644m**

R56

Picnic

Melrose
Ryno

R56

Ryno

Cicira

Mzwazwa

R56

21

Sunnyside

7

Naver

8

Ulin
▲ **1444m**

Cala
Road

Crimora

Keifas

Xalanga

5

Qiba

Blomvlei

Kannaskop
▲ **1681m**

Tshukutshesi

Chibini

▲ **1596m**

Fairview

Keppoch

Galili

22

The Glen

R58

KuKowa

Siginqini

14

Waterlea

Ncongu

Spitskop

St Gabriel

Cala Pass

Oakville

Sifondile

45

Taynult

Peninsula

Cala

Kwezi

Aultbea

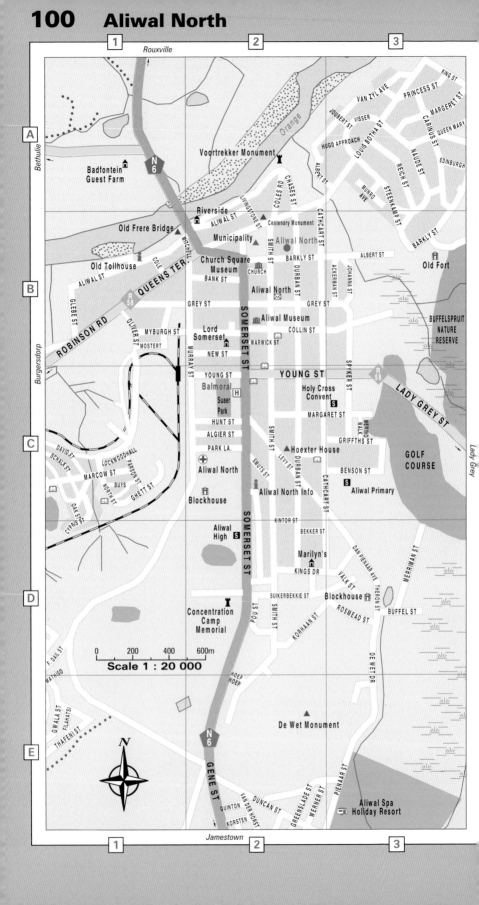

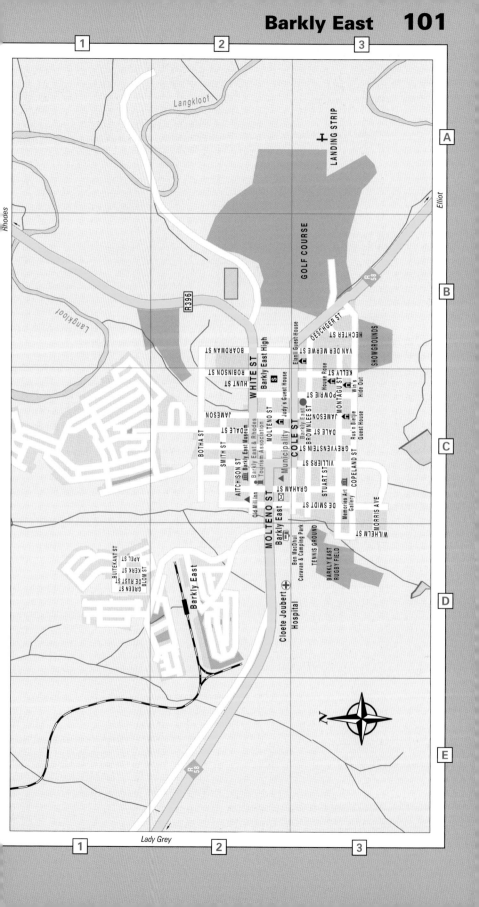

Langkloof

LANDING STRIP

Rhodes

GOLF COURSE

Elliot

Langkloof

R396

SHOWGROUNDS

R 58

DESCHGER ST

HECHTER ST

VAN DER MERWE ST

BOARDMAN ST

WHITE ST

Barkly East High

Elani Guest House

HUNT ST

ROBINSON ST

KELLY ST

House Rose

JAMESON

MOLTENO ST

Judy's Guest House

POWRIE ST

MONTAGU ST

Win s
Hide Out

Barkly East

COLE ST

BROWNLEE ST

JAMESON ST

Barkly East & Rhodes
Tourism Association

Rus n Bietjie
Guest House

Barkly East Museum

DALE ST

BOTHA ST

SMITH ST

AITCHISON ST

Municipality

GREVENSTEIN ST

DALE ST

VILLIERS ST

COPELAND ST

Old Mill Inn

MOLTENO ST

STUART ST

GRAHAM ST

DE SMIDT ST

Memories Art
Gallery

MORRIS AVE

Barkly East

Ben MacDhui
Caravan & Camping Park

TENNIS GROUND

BARKLY EAST
RUGBY FIELD

WILHELM ST

BUITEKANT ST

APEL ST

GREEN ST

DE RUST ST

KERK ST

BLOM ST

Barkly East

Cloete Joubert
Hospital

R 58

Lady Grey

N

A

B

C

D

E

Aliwal North

1   **2**   **3**

N

A

Venterstad

**BURGERSDORP
GOLF COURSE**

R 58

Blockhouse

Burgersdorp

Old Gaol

The Nook B&B

B

R 58

MAASDORP ST

BREBNER ST

CORMACK ST

PRES.SWART RD

FINCHAM ST

DANIE BUTLER CR

STORMBERG AVE

SPRUIT AVE

MULLER ST

LOUIS VORSTER

HARMONIE RD

Dusk to Dawn
Guest House

VILJOEN ST

VAN DER WALT ST

PIET RETIEF ST

KERK ST

PRES.SWART RD

MURRAY ST

HOPLEY ST

Rehobot G H

The Hut B&B

37 V.D.Walt Guest House

Burgersdorp Museum

DAANTJIE VAN DENHEEVER RD

Burgersdorp Hospital

7TH AVE

1ST AVE

HOSPITAL ST

TAYLOR ST

HENDRICK POTGIETER RD

BUITENKANT ST

BIRD ST

Burger Square

Burgersdorp

JAN GREYLING ST

SMITH ST

ROCHELLE ST

NAVARRE ST

NGK

9TH AVE

10TH AVE

11TH AVE

12TH AVE

13TH AVE

MONUMENT ST

POSTMA ST

SINTON ST

PARK AVE

2ND AVE

3RD AVE

4TH AVE

5TH AVE

JOTHAM JOUBERT ST

SCOLIGNY ST

Burgersdorp Lodge/Jubilee Lodge

Burgersdorp

KLOOF ST

SPOORWEG ST

Municipality

Tombstone
Prof.D.Postma

C

MERINO ST

6TH AVE

MERINO ST

JUKES KNIGHT ST

SHORTEN ST

SCHWEIZER ST

QUEEN ST

Jamestown

LEEUWBEKKIE ST

TULP ST

ASTER ST

ANGELIER ST

YGIE ST

EUREKA

FRANS COETZEE ST

STEPHANUS VAN WYK ST

PAUL GROBLER ST

R391

MZAMOMHLE

D

E

QUEENSTOWN RD

Molteno

1   **2**   **3**

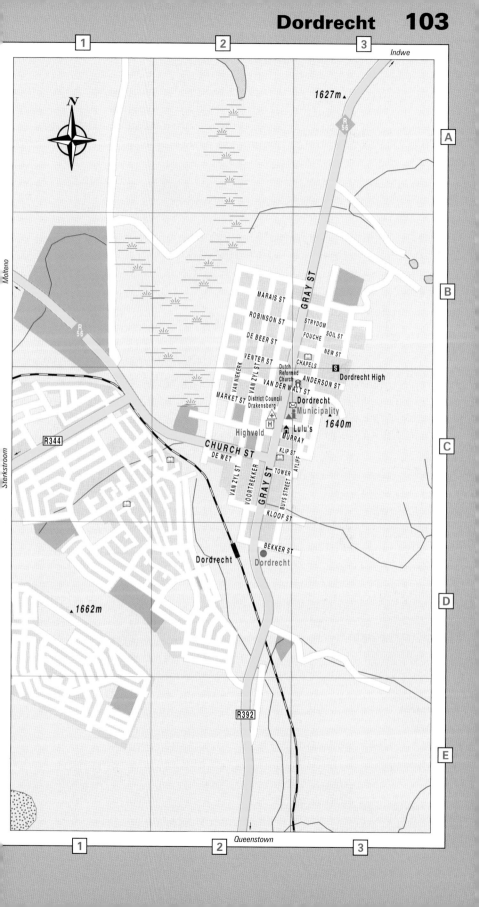

Indwe

1627m ▲

1640m

1662m ▲

Molteno

Sterkstroom

R56

R344

R392

R56

GRAY ST

MARAIS ST

ROBINSON ST

DE BEER ST

VENTER ST

MARKET ST

VAN NIEKERK

VAN ZYL ST

VAN DER WALT ST

STRYDOM

FOUCHE

SOIL ST

NEW ST

CHAPELS

ANDERSON ST

Dutch Reformed Church

Dordrecht High

S

Dordrecht Municipality

District Council Drakensberg

H

Highveld

Lulu's

MURRAY

CHURCH ST

DE WET

VAN ZYL ST

VOORTREKKER

GRAY ST

KLIP ST

AYLIFF

TOWER

BUY'S STREET

KLOOF ST

BEKKER ST

Dordrecht

Dordrecht

Queenstown

1   2   3

A

B

C

D

E

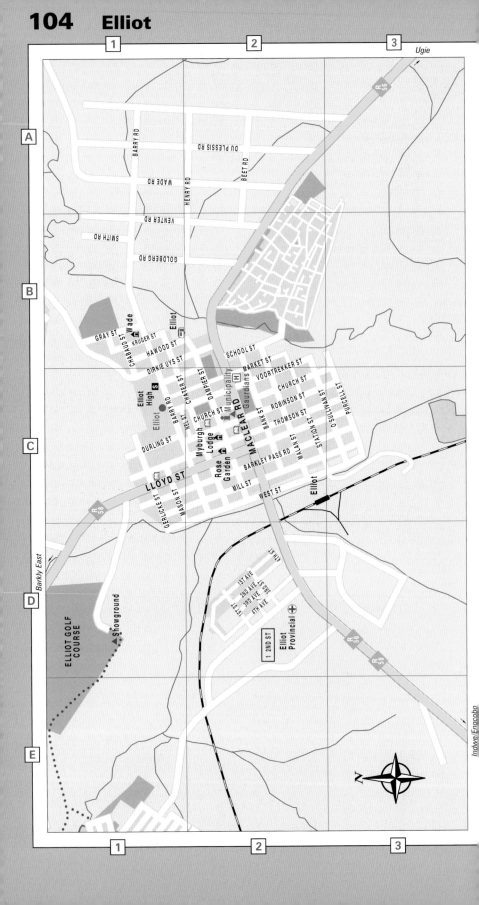

Ugie

Barkly East

Indwe/Enacobo

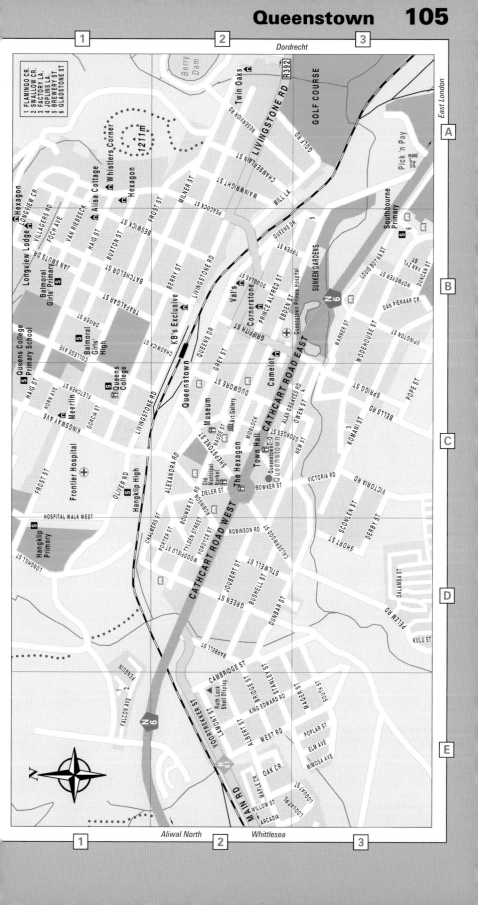

Wild Coast Wild Coast Wild C

As befits a region known as The Wild Coast, this spectacular coastline is as close to an untouched paradise as you could wish for, with undeveloped coastline and beaches stretching for mile upon mile. This unique area is also the keeper of a great many 'hidden secrets', with all the adventure opportunities you could ask for as well as a bounty of fish to be hooked (over 800 species nibble off the coast). The birdlife is exceptional, while the rural areas continue to nurture and grow the age-old Xhosa traditions and customs. Spend too much time on the Wild Coast and you'll be in danger of changing your way of thinking (and living!) forever.

42	Tourist region maps and town plans
32	Chapter opener maps
◉	Point of interest

N1

Colesberg ◉

R5

N10   **N9**

Northern Cape

N1   **R56**

Richmond   Middelburg ◉

WILD COAST WILDLIFE

Cape Clawless Otter in Cwebe NR.
Wide range of game in Nduli NR.
Red hartbeest, Stanley Bustard and other game and birds in Luchaba NR.
Blesbuck, Burchell's zebra and blue wildebeest in Silaka NR
Sea birds on Bird Island (near Silaka NR).
Most of the above animals, as well as blesbuck, monitor lizards, long crested eagles, African jacana and yellow-throated longclaw in Hluleka NR.

Western Cape

R63

Cradock ◉

Graaff-Reinet ◉ ◉

Mountain Zebra National Park ◉

Karoo Nature Reserve

N1

Pearston ◉

N9   **R63**

R75   Somerset East ◉

Addo Elephant National Park ◉

Sundays River Valley   Sha Game R

Baviaanskloof Wilderness Areas   Uitenhage ◉

R62   Joubertina ◉   Jeffreys Bay ◉

Kareedouw ◉   PORT

N2   ELIZABETH ◉

Tsitsikamma National Park   Humansdorp ◉ ◉   Summerstran

St Francis Bay

WILD COAST ICONS

The dramatic Hole-in-the-Wall near Coffee Bay.
Nelson Mandela's birthplace - the village of Quna.
The Nelson Mandela Museum and the Transkei Museum in Umtata.

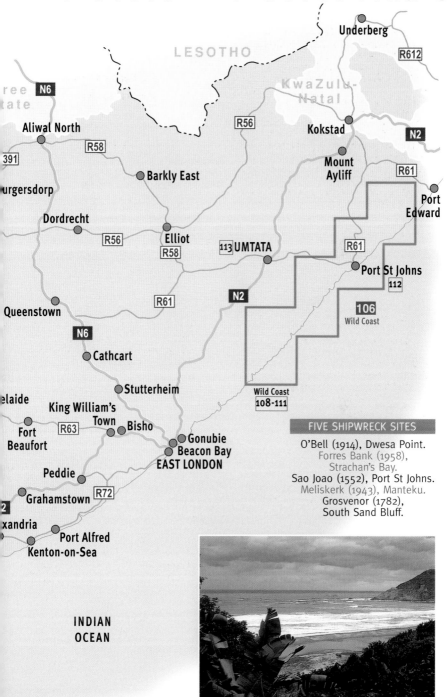

Wild Coast Wild Coast Wild C

Underberg

R612

LESOTHO

KwaZulu-Natal

N6

ree
tate

R56

Aliwal North

Kokstad

N2

R58

391

Mount
Ayliff

Barkly East

R61

urgersdorp

Port
Edward

Dordrecht

R56

Elliot

113 UMTATA

R61

R58

Port St Johns

112

Queenstown

R61

N2

106
Wild Coast

N6

Cathcart

Stutterheim

Wild Coast
108-111

elaide

King William's
Town

Bisho

FIVE SHIPWRECK SITES

Fort
Beaufort

R63

Gonubie

O'Bell (1914), Dwesa Point.
Forres Bank (1958),
Strachan's Bay.
Sao Joao (1552), Port St Johns.
Meliskerk (1943), Manteku.
Grosvenor (1782),
South Sand Bluff.

Beacon Bay

EAST LONDON

Peddie

Grahamstown

R72

xandria

Port Alfred

Kenton-on-Sea

INDIAN
OCEAN

Sea view at Port St Johns.

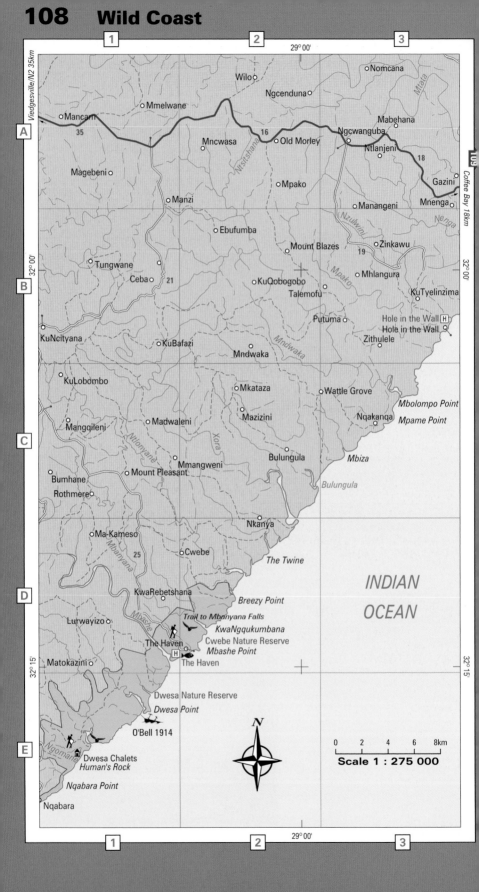

4 • 29° 15' • 5 Umtata 62km • 6

Ngqumani

Dangwana

Ngqongweni

Mngazana

Glengazi

Bizana

Lokweni

Port St. Johns 25km

Libode 20km

20

Baca

Mdumazulu

Ngwane

Ludalasio

62

R 61

25

Tombo

Mngazi

A

110

KwaMaye

Old Bunting

Tyelimanzi
495m

Buto

Bholanio

KwaGulwa

Kwanyana

Umngazane

Zinduneni

Zingosini

20

Noxovao

*Boulder
Bay*

*Brazen
Head*

Ntatweni

Notintsila

Sankobe

Mpamba

Nyakani

Mpande

KuRebu

B

31° 45'

Sidanda

Qokama

Ntsundwane

Mtakatye

Myila

KwaDiko

Sharks Point

31° 45'

10

KwaMjanyane

Mtonga
Rame Head

Lower Rainy

Mngampunzi

Mnenu

9

Mgoqweni

Hluleke

Hluleka Nature Reserve

Ku-Ngodo

Mzonyane

5

5

Banana Bay

Nkweleni

Strachan's Bay

C

Mtakatyi

5

Ntsimbini

Lwandile

Forres Bank 1958

9

9

Mdumbi

Presley's Bay

Presley Bay

Ntshilini

Ndungunyeni

Mtata

Lutsheni

D

Gazini

8

2

Tshani

N

69

Mnenga

Anchorage

H

Whale Rock

Mtata

108

Sizendeni

6

Umtata Mouth

Nenga

Maphuzi Point

32° 00'

Coffee Bay

H

Coffee Bay

Ocean View

Mhulungwana Point

INDIAN

32° 00'

Hole in the Wall

H

Black Rock

Hole in the Wall

Hole in the Wall

OCEAN

E

4 • 29° 15' • 5 • 6

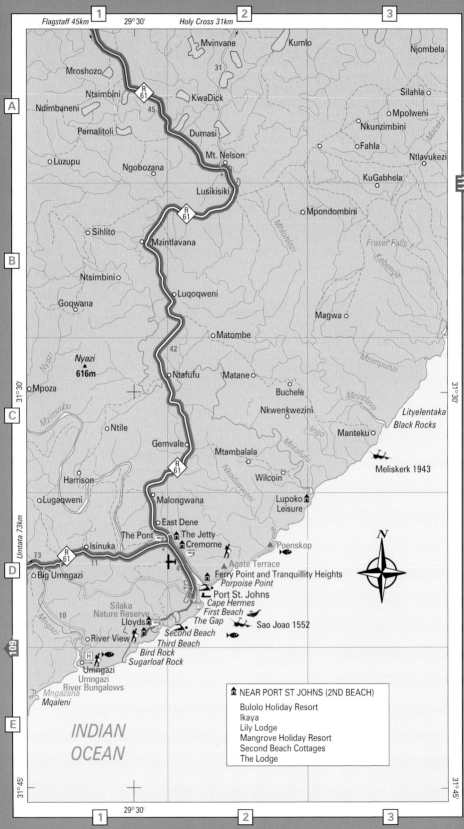

1　**2**　**3**

111

A

Mroshozo
Ntsimbini
Ndimbaneni
Pamalitoli
Luzupu
Ngobozana

Mvinvane
Kumlo
Njombela
KwaDick
Silahla
Mpolweni
Nkunzimbini
Fahla
Ntlavukezi
KuGabhela

R61
45
31
Dumasi
Mt. Nelson
Lusikisiki

B

Sihlito
Ntsimbini
Goqwana

Mzintlavana
Luqoqweni
Matombe

Mpondombini
Fraser Falls
Magwa

R61

31° 30'

C

Mpoza
Nyazi
616m
Ntile
Harrison
Lugaqweni

Ntafufu
Matane
Buchele
Nkwenkwezini
Gemvale
Mtambalala
Wilcoin
Manteku

Lityelentaka
Black Rocks
Meliskerk 1943

42
R61

31° 30'

D

Umtata 73km
Big Umngazi
Isinuka
The Pont
East Dene
Malongwana

73
11
R61
4
The Jetty
Cremorne
Ferry Point and Tranquillity Heights
Porpoise Point
Port St. Johns
Cape Hermes
First Beach
The Gap
Sao Joao 1552

Poenskop
Agate Terrace

Lupoko
Leisure

N

Silaka
Nature Reserve
Lloyds
River View
Umngazi
Umngazi
River Bungalows
Mqaleni

Second Beach
Third Beach
Bird Rock
Sugarloaf Rock

109

E

INDIAN
OCEAN

🏠 NEAR PORT ST JOHNS (2ND BEACH)

Bulolo Holiday Resort
Ikaya
Lily Lodge
Mangrove Holiday Resort
Second Beach Cottages
The Lodge

29° 45' Bizana 36km
30° 00' Bizana 56km

Port Edward 56km

56

Mahlaba

Mjela

Mgeni

Sidinga

Gumzana

Lukayisweni

Mbongweni

Mzamba

Njasitube

Njana

A

36

Kanyayo

Spes Bona

Silinjana

Nthlahlane

Zangotsho

B

36

Kanya

Hlabatini

39

Mseleni

Flagstaff 36km

Flagstaff 39km

31° 15'

Mkamela

28

Mkambati
Nature
Reserve

Mtentu

C

31° 15'

Tanga

Mkambati

Mkambati
Horseshoe

Njombela

Lupondo

Msikaba

Gwe-Gwe

Mkambati
Palms

Ntentula

Mkambati

Mateku

Matewu

Ndindindi

Mbaxeni

South Sand
Bluff

Grosvenor 1782

D

518m
Kwabonomaza

Tezana

Kilroe Beach

Port Grosvenor

Lambasi Bay

Mkweni

Lupatana

Goss Point

Cutweni

Mfihlelo

Mlambomkulu

Luphuthana

*Top Hat
Waterfall Bluff*

N

E

Mfihlelo

Myekane

Cathedral
Rock

Mbotyi
Montshe
Mzimpunzi

INDIAN
OCEAN

29° 45'

30° 00'

Umtata/Lusikisiki

1 2 3

N

A

Eagles Nest
168m

190m

Ferry Point Rd

Mzimvubu

Coastal Needles

Dick King Plaque

H

Ferry Point
Tranquility
Heights

Ferry

18m

Poenskop

KLOOF ST

WESTGATE ST
GARDEN ST

VICTORIA ST

NORTH ST

BRIDGE ST

Port St. Johns RC.
Secondary

S

Faranani Guest House

Municipality

Port St. Johns

Outspan Inn

Agate Terrace

B

Umtata/Airfield

WEST ST

CHURCH ST

BEACH RD

ALBERT ST

HERMES ST

MAIN ST

BEREA RD

MARINE DR

HERMES RD

Port St.Johns Secondary

S

Gwyneth's Barn

CEMETERY

Umzimvubu
Retreat Guest House

Port St. Johns

PETTY COAT LA.

First Beach

C

Wild Coast Guest House

PORT ST. JOHNS
GOLF COURSE

GOLF COURSE DR

Cape Hermes

CEMETERY

Sunlof B&B

First Beach
Camp

131m

A

D

SECOND BEACH RD

148m

Second Beach/Silaka Nature Reserve

MTUMBANE

The Gap

E

INDIAN OCEAN

0   200   400   600m

Scale 1 : 20 000

Port St Johns

Mount Frere

St Johns College

St Johns
College

RICHMOND ST

OXLAND ST

CALLAWAY ST

EAGLE ST

Excelsior Secondary

BARST

GOITA ST

CATHAM ST

SPRIGG

Protea

N2

Transkei

BRIDGE ST

ELLIOT RD

MADEIRA RD

YORK ST

Nelson Mandela Museum

Umtata

KLETTE ST

Norwood Secondary

WADDELL ST

2ND AVE

HEATHCOTE

1ST AVE

3RD AVE

St Joseph's Secondary

4TH AVE

HARROW ST

OWEN ST

Umtata

OWEN ST

HOSTELS

Umtata

5TH AVE

6TH AVE

CASSEL ST

Royal

Holy Cross Secondary

Leeds Rd

St Mary's Hospital

Umtata High

NELSON MANDELA DR.

KING EDWARD

ZIGZAG ST

CRAISTER ST

VICTORIA ST

Transkei Primary

BEAUFORT ST

SUTHERLAND ST

SAVOY ST

WESLEY ST

STANFORD TER

LOWRY

HEMING

PARK

N2

ZANEMALI RD

Umtata

CUMBERLAND ST

DEVILLE RD

BLAKEWAY ST

HOSPITAL RD

HUGHES

PRESTWICH

NEPGEN AVE

UMTATA COUNTRY CLUB

R61

Umtata

PINE TREE

HIBISCUS

ERICA

UMBENGE

TECOMA

Sir Henry Elliot Hospital

Northcrest Secondary

DANGERFIELD

MILLAR

NELSON

YELLOWWOOD

CHESTNUT

POPLAR

KIEPERSOL

Umtata General Hospital

Tipini Secondary

NELSON MANDELA DR.

JASMINE DR

CYPRESS DR

EBONY RD

BLUEGUM RD

SISSON ST

NDULI CRES

ERIC SPILKEN ST

DON THOMPSON DR

MIMOSA

WILLOW DR

ORCHID ST

PROTEA

ALOE ST

TULIP

DAISY

LILY

SISSON ST

ROSE

CANNNA

AIREY

TERRANCE LOWRY ST

Owen Dam

NDULI NATURE RESERVE

N

R61

N2

DURROW ST

KNOPF ST

Engcobo

Idutywa

Index Index Index Index Index In

Index Index Index Index Index In

Index Index Index Index Index In

Index Index Index Index Index In

ndex Index Index Index Index Inde

Index Index Index Index Index In

Resources Resources Resources R

EASTERN CAPE CONTACT DETAILS & INFORMATION

The following telephone numbers (and cyber connections) are as correct as possible at time of going to print. Numbers and codes do change over time, as do the names of establishments. For any queries dial 1023 (telephone enquiries), 10118 (talking yellow pages) or visit www.yellowpages.co.za (electronic yellow pages). NOTE: numbers listed are all phone numbers – no fax numbers or physical addresses are provided here.

A place where you can enjoy 9 tourist routes in a malaria free environment

Useful Numbers
SA National Parks (Pretoria) 012 428 9111
General Directory Enquiries 1023
International Enquiries 0903
Telkom Information Centre 080 111 1189
Police 10111
Ambulance 10177
AA Breakdown 0800 010 177

Cellular Emergencies
Cell-C 084140
MTN 112
Vodacom 147

Money Matters
American Express 011 359 0111
Diners Club 011 358 8400
Mastercard International 0800 990 418
Visa International 0800 990475
Thomas Cook Rennies 0800 998 175
Europ Assistance 011 254 1000

Major Towns in the Eastern Cape
Aliwal North
Cradock
East London
Graaff-Reinet
Grahamstown
King William's Town
Port Alfred
Port Elizabeth
Queenstown
Somerset East
Uitenhage
Umtata

9 TOURIST ROUTES TO EXPLORE
Tsitsikamma 042 280 3561
www.tsitsikamma.net

Kouga Region 042 293 2923
www.jeffreysbaytourism.com

Sundays River Valley Route 042 233 0040
www.sundaysrivervalley.com

Sunshine Coast Tourism 046 648 2418
www.kenton.co.za

Karoo Heartland 049 892 4248
www.graaffreinet.co.za

Frontier Country 046 622 3241
www.grahamstown.co.za

Amatola Mountains Escape 045 962 1340

Friendly N6 051 633 3567
www.ectourism.co.za

Wild Coast 047 531 5290 / 2
www.ectourism.co.za

Tourist Boards and Bodies
Eastern Cape Tourism Board 043 701 9600
www.ectourism.co.za, info@ectourism.co.za

Eastern Cape Tourism (Umtata) 047 531 5290/2
ectbwc@ectourism.co.za, www.ectourism.co.za

Tourist Information Centre Port Elizabeth
Nelson Mandela Bay Tourism
041 583 2030, www.eascapism.com

ECTOUR 041 507 7912
ectour@sunint.co.za, www.eascapism.co.za

South African Tourism (H / O) 011 778 8000

Resources Resources Resources

Tourist Offices

Aberdeen Municipality 049 846 0014
Adelaide Municipality 046 684 0034 / 0177
Alexandria Tourism 046 624 1235, 648 2418
Alice 046 645 7454
Alicedale Info Bushman Sand Day Centre
042 231 1350, 231 1013
Aliwal North 051 633 3567
ectban@intekom.co.za, www.ectourism.co.za
Amatola District Municipality 043 701 4000
mpumif@amatoladm.co.za
Bathurst-Ndlambe Tourism Port Alfred Unit
046 624 1235, 625 0639
www.port-alfred.co.za, tourism@ndlambe.co.za
Bedford Community Tourism Organization
046 785 0680, 685 0076
kim@bedfordproperty.co.za
Buffalo City 043 722 6015
www.visitbuffalocity.co.za
info@tourismbuffalocity.co.za
Burgersdorp Community Tourism Office
051 653 1752 / 0086
Cathcart Community Tourism Office
045 843 1022, 072 406 4185
Cradock Tourism 048 881 2383
www.cradock.co.za
Cookhouse Municipality 042 247 1166
Info Somerset East 042 243 1333
Despatch Municipality 041 933 1111
Info Despatch Library 041 994 1616
Dordrecht Tourism 045 941 1014 / 1030
Elliot Municipality 045 931 1011, 082 701 7754
Engcobo 047 548 1221
Fort Beaufort-Kat River Community Tourism
Office 046 645 1555 (Library)
Graaff-Reinet Publicity 049 892 4248
info@graaffreinet.co.za, www.graaffreinet.co.za
Grahamstown Tourism 046 622 3241
info@grahamstown.co.za
www.grahamstown.co.za
Hankey Tourism 042 284 0543
Herschel Tourism Sterkspruit
051 611 0031 / 0065
Hagmorkei (Haga-Haga, Morgan Bay, Kei
Mouth) 043 841 1645 / 1062
mb.hotel@mweb.co.za
Hofmeyr Municipality 048 885 0097
082 777 4482
Hogsback Tourism (Amatola Mountain Escape
Tourist Information Office) 045 962 1340 /
1130, 082 433 1538, 084 752 7958
Humansdorp Tourism 042 295 1361
Jamestown Municipality 051 641 0641

Jansenville Publicity 049 836 0021
Kareedouw Publicity 042 288 0303
Jeffreys Bay Tourism
042 293 2923, 293 2588
Jbay-tourism@agnet.co.za
www.jeffreysbaytourism.com
Kei Bridge Information 043 831 2004
Kei District Council 047 501 6400
Keiskammahoek Municipality 040 658 0028
Kenton-on-Sea / Bushmans Publicity
046 648 2418, kentoninfo@telkomsa.net
www.kenton.co.za
King William's Town Community Tourism Office
043 642 3391 info@tourismbuffalocity.co.za
www.visitbuffalocity.co.za
Lady Frere Municipality 047 878 0020
Lady Grey Community Tourism Office
051 603 0176 / 0407 / 1114
Langkloof Tourism 042 273 1065, 273 1516
Maclear / Ugie Community Tourism Office
045 933 1335 / 7 petebaum@xsinet.co.za
Middelburg Karoo Publicity 049 842 2188
tourismmid@adsactive.com
www.middelburgec.co.za
Molteno Community Tourism Organization
045 969 0251, 967 0021
Nelson Mandela Bay Tourism (Port Elizabeth)
041 585 8884 info@nmbt.co.za
www.nmbt.co.za
Nieu-Bethesda Publicity 049 841 1659
Patensie / Greater Baviaanskloof
042 283 0437
Tolbos Country Shop & Restaurant
info@baviaans.net, www.baviaans.net
Port Alfred Tourism 046 624 1235
patourism@intekom.co.za
tourism@ndlambe.co.za, www.port-alfred.co.za
Port Elizabeth (see Nelson Mandela Bay Tourism)
Port St Francis 042 294 0150
portstfrancis@intekom.co.za
www.portstfrancis.co.za
Port St Johns Tourism 047 564 1187, 1207/8
tourismpsj@wildcoast.co.za
www.portstjohns.org.za/tourism
Queenstown Information Office 045 839 2265
sarto@eci.co.za
Rhodes Tourism 045 974 9305
www.rhodesvillage.co.za
St Francis Bay Tourism 042 294 0076
Info@stfrancistourism.co.za
www.stfrancistourism.co.za
Steynsburg Community Tourism Office
048 884 0034

Steytlerville Baviaans Tourist Route
049 835 0022 / 0153
Somerset East Bluecrane Tourism
042 243 1448 / 1333
bluecranetourism@isat.co.za
www.somerseteast.co.za
Stutterheim Development Foundation
043 683 2024
Sundays River Valley Publicity
(Greater Addo/Paterson) 042 233 0040
peter.burton@absamail.co.za
www.sundaysrivervalley.com
Tarkastad Community Tourism Office
045 846 0324 / 0410 / 0199
bandpking@worldonline.co.za
tarkatic@telkomsa.net
Tsitsikamma Tourism Information
042 280 3561, 281 1849
adventure@gardenroute.co.za
www.tsitsikamma.net
Uitenhage Municipality 041 994 1408
Ukhlamba Tourism Association
039 737 4176, 082 489 2117 uta@icon.co.za
Umtata Wild Coast Tourism
047 531 5290 / 2
ectbwc@ectourism.co.za, www.ectourism.co.za
Venterstad Community Tourism Office
051 654 0150, 0024 / 5
gfontein@kingsley.co.za
Wild Coast District Council 039 254 0320
Willowmore Municipality 044 923 1004
www.baviaans.co.za

TRANSPORT
Countrywide Airport Information
Johannesburg International Airport
Arrival & Departure Enquiries 011 921 6262
Bloemfontein 051 433 2901
Cape Town International Airport 021 937 1200
Central Reservations 011 978 1111
Durban International Airport 031 451 6666
George 044 876 9310
SA Express 011 978 5569
Umtata Airport 047 536 0023
Weatherline 082 162

East London Airport Information
Air Carrier & Charter Operator
043 736 2688, 736 1663
082 339 4589, 082 339 4590
East London 043 706 0306
SAA East London 043 700 1111

Port Elizabeth Airport Information
General Information 041 507 7319 / 7201
SAA Port Elizabeth 041 507 7204
Reservations 041 507 1111
Nationwide 041 507 7281
SA Airlink 041 581 6608
BA Comair 041 508 8099
Sheltam Aviation 041 581 4194 / 5 / 6
Air Moves 042 294 1241

Portnet (harbour information & authority)
East London 043 700 1185
Port Elizabeth 041 507 1800 / 2662

Rail (through Spoortnet)
Shosholoza Meyl Trains 041 507 2662
Central Reservations 086 000 8888
www.spoornet.co.za

Road Information
Speed limit on freeways is 120km/h unless
otherwise indicated: 80km/h on urban
freeways, 60km/h in built up areas. Road
signages along the roads in accordance with
international codes. Foreign tourists require
an international driver's licence. The legal
blood /alcohol limit 0.05mg per 100ml.

Traffic Department H/O Eastern Cape
043 705 9333, 705 9302

Car Hire / Rentals
Avis-Rent-a-Car 086 102 1111
Hertz Reservations 0861 1600 136
National Car Rentals 0800 01 13 23
Budget Rent-a-Car 046 624 2099

Car Hire in Port Elizabeth
Avis 041 581 4291, 501 7200
Budget Rent-a-Car 041 581 4242 / 82
Economic 041 581 5826, 082 800 4258
Imperial 041 581 1268 / 4214
National Car Rental 041 581 1123
Tempest Car Hire 041 581 1256

Car Hire in East London
Avis Rent-a-Car 043 727 1324
Airport 043 736 2250
Budget Car Rental 043 736 2364
Airport 043 736 1084
Imperial 043 734 2230
National Car Rental 043 736 2900

Resources Resources Resources

INTERCITY BUS SERVICES
Baz Bus
East London-Port Elizabeth &
East London-Durban 021 439 2323
City to City 041 392 1333
Intercape Mainliner
Port Elizabeth 0861 287 287
East London 043 726 9580
Greyhound Intercity Coach
Port Elizabeth 041 363 4555
East London 043 743 9284
Translux
Port Elizabeth 041 392 1333
East London 043 700 1999, 700 1014
J-Bay Sunshine Express
042 293 2221, 082 956 2687
Mini-Lux East London
043 741 3107, 741 1310, 083 300 5244
SA Connections
043 722 0284, 743 0156
Sunshine Passenger Services
Port Elizabeth 082 956 2687, 042 293 1911

Shuttle Services
East Coast Shuttle Services
043 740 5718, 083 449 2974
East London Backpackers Shuttle Services
043 722 2748
Eastern Cape Airport Shuttle Services
043 748 3883, 082 663 3087

ADVENTURES, ACTIVITIES & ENTERTAINMENT
Biking
Graaff-Reinet 049 892 4248
Hogsback Mountain Bike Trail 045 962 1069
Nieu-Bethesda Hire a Bike 049 841 1642
Port Elizabeth Longmore Forest Mountain Bike
Trail & Baakens River Mountain Bike Trail
041 583 2030
Rhodes Mountain Biking 045 974 9305

Bird Watching
Barkly East Bird Club
045 971 0016, 082 929 1512
Gonubie Nature Reserve
043 740 4000, 741 2212
Graaff-Reinet Bird Club 049 891 0353
Jeffreys Bay Tourism (Kabeljou Nature Reserve,
Seekoei River Nature Reserve, the Noorsekloof
& Paradise Beach) 042 293 2923
Port Elizabeth Eastern Cape Wild Bird Society
041 360 4245, 083 659 2192

Dolphin & Whale Watching
Port St Johns 082 783 1288

Entertainment in Port Elizabeth
The Boardwalk Casino & Entertainment World
041 507 7777, boardwalk@sunint.co.za,
www.boardwalk.co.za

Fishing
East London Deep Sea Fishing
043 735 2604
Port St Johns Fly Fishing
083 775 2082
Rhodes Wild Trout Association
045 974 9290
Wild Cat Fishing Charters, Deep Sea Game
Fishing Adventures
082 654 9629

Haunted Walks
Port Elizabeth 041 583 2584

Hiking
Port St Johns 082 507 2256

Horse trails
Guided Horse Trails & Gamedrives
042 233 0556
St Francis Bay Oyster Bay Lodge
042 297 0150

Hunting
Eastern Cape Tourism Board 040 635 2115

Mountain Climbing
Nieu-Bethesda 049 841 1635
Port Elizabeth Mountain Club of South Africa
041 365 5543

Sand Boarding
Aloe Afrika Adventures
042 296 2974, 293 3941

4x4 Adventures
Port St Johns 082 783 1288

Tour Operators

Alan Weyers Historical Day Tours, Frontier Country 046 622 7896
info@alanweyerstours.co.za
Algoa Tours, Port Elizabeth 041 581 2403
info@algoatours.com
Aloe Africa, Jeffreys Bay 042 296 2974
Amadiba Adventures 039 305 6455 / 7
Amahlati Excursions, Grahamstown
046 622 4517, 083 631 4800
www.grahamstown.co.za/amahlati
Amanzi River Rafters, Cradock
048 881 2976 / 082 894 2873
amanzi@intekom.co.za
Amanzi Tours 041371 4665
amanzi@everywhere.co.za
www.amanzitours.co.za
Amatola Tours, Port Elizabeth 041 581 7780
info@amatour.co.za, www.touringsa.co.za
Awesome Africa Tours & Adventures
041 374 8766, danny@awesomeafrica.co.za
www.awesomeafrica.co.za
Bay Tourism, Port Elizabeth 041 584 0622
nikki@baytours.co.za, gary@baytours.co.za
Bees Tours, Grahamstown 046 622 5051
Beyond Adventures 043 743 5778
www.beyondadventure.co.za
Birdwatching & Eco Tours 041 466 5698
info@birdtours.co.za, www.birdtours.co.za
Bukani Travel & Tours
041 464 7812, 083 657 2666
C&Z Tours, Alice 083 360 2417
Calabash Tours, Port Elizabeth 041 585 6162
calabash@iafrica.com
Chalani Tours, Graaff-Reinet
049 892 2893, 083 305 9923
Charter Flights, East London Air 043 736 1663
airhart@iafrica.com
Dtours, Tarkastad 045 848 0152
Friendly City Tours (Port Elizabeth)
041 585 1801, alandickinson@webmail.co.za
Frontier Country Connections, Grahamstown
046 622 8054, info@frontiercountry.co.za
www.frontiercountry.co.za
Fundani Township Tours, Port Elizabeth
041 454 2064 / 7, cultours@iafrica.com
Gateway Tour Centre, Port Elizabeth
041 582 2833, nick@epweb.co.za
Golf n Game, Port Elizabeth
041 373 3092, 082 930 0768
golfngame@telkomsa.net, www.golfngame.co.za
Helicopter Flips 041 582 2597, 082 774 3553
www.aw8helicopters.co.za

Heritage Tours, Jeffreys Bay 041 582 3216
cmiddle@iafrica.com
Imandi Tours, East London
083 307 5682, 043 734 3663
info@imandi.co.za, www.imandi.co.za
Imonti Tours, East London
083 487 8975, 043 741 3884
imontitours@sainet.co.za
Indudumo Ventures, Port Elizabeth
041 378 1418, 082 265 5489, 082 890 4281
davidv@zipips.co.za
Jarandi Tours & Safaris, Port Elizabeth
082 295 9521
safari@jarandi.com, www.jarandi.com
J'Bay Surf Tours, Jeffreys Bay 042 293 3304
sarah@egent.co.za
Karoo Connections Tours & Safaris,
Graaff-Reinet 049 892 3978
karooconnection@intekom.co.za
Karoo Experience Tours, Middelburg
049 842 1790, 073 224 0759
www.karoolodge.co.za
Kyalami Tours, Port Elizabeth 082 485 2759
kayalami@webmail.com
Kelly's Tours, Port Elizabeth
046 648 2545, 082 450 7771
Kwanti Safaris, Port Elizabeth 082 551 5752
jeand@mweb.co.za, www.kwantisafaris.co.za
Let's Go Tours, Port Alfred 046 624 1866
082 966 1762, 072 447 4801
jawa@border.co.za
www.comfycorner-letsgotours.co.za
Littlejohn Cruises, Port Elizabeth
041 586 1689, 082 577 0240
Lynx Tours, Jeffreys Bay 042 296 0594 / 2563
info@lynx-tours.com
Maximum Exposure Adventure, Port Alfred
046 624 4432, 082 692 6189
Ngonyama Tour Adventure, Port Elizabeth
041 396 0575, 083 757 8163
admin@ngonyama.za.net
www.ngonyama.za.net
Pembury Tours, Port Elizabeth 041 581 2581
Pineapple Factory Tours, East London
043 731 1770 (closed mid-Dec to end Jan)
Reefocean Tours, East London 043 722 3239
shaneainslie@lantic.net, www.reefocean-tours.co.za
Real Cape Adventures 042 293 3719
Ross Tours, Port Elizabeth 041 581 3223
Saunter Tours, Port Elizabeth 041 366 1315
janpatti@global.co.za

Resources Resources Resources

Sekhanya Tours, Jeffreys Bay 082 701 7277
Share Tours CC, Port Elizabeth
041 365 0536, 083 655 9072
andr@freemail.absa.co.za
Shumba Safaris, Hankey 082 576 2642
adolfkleinhans@capevalleysafaris.co.za
Shield Tours, Port Elizabeth 041 367 3868
Sights & Sounds, Port Elizabeth 041 367 3058
Speirs Tours, East London 043 642 1747
info@speirstours.co.za, www.speirtours.co.za
Southern Cross Safaris, Cradock
048 886 0606, 082 455 2643
southern-cross@intekom.co.za
www.southern-cross-safaris.co.za
Springbok Atlas, Port Elizabeth 041 581 2555
isabella@springbokatlas.com
Storms River Adventures, Tsitsikamma
042 541 1609
Stormsriver adventures 042 281 1836
www.stormsriver.com
Sunshine Excursions, Port Elizabeth
041 373 7023, 082 564 2338
Sunshine Express, Jeffreys Bay 042 293 2221
Swartkei Safaris Tarkastad
040 845 1100, 082 652 5320
info@swartkeisafaris.com
Tanaqua Indigenous Tours, Port Elizabeth
083 270 9924, 083 995 6345
tanaquatours@wol.co.za
Thula Tours, Port Elizabeth
041 379 4214, 082 410 8840
thebayop@mweb.co.za
Touring Agencies, Butterworth 043 726 2669
True African Tours, Hankey
042 284 0543, 042 284 0878
Turaco Tours, Port Elizabeth
041 365 4838, 082 784 3242
turacotours@mweb.co.za, www.turacotours.com
Turquoise Horizen, East London 043 748 6128
thorizen@iafrica.com
Tsitsikamma Canopy Tours 042 281 1836
info@treetoptour.com, www.treetoptour.com
Outdoor Magic 041 581 8795, 082 960 9262
Umzantsi Africa, Port Elizabeth
041 364 2673, 082 361 9733, 082 822 4717
denpete@mweb.co.za
Wilderness & Coastal Tours, King William's
Town 043 642 4973
Xhosaland Tourism, East London
083 548 0317, xhosalandtourism@telkomsa.net
www.xhosalandtourism.com
YQK Tours, Alice 082 400 3911

18-Hole Golf Courses in the Eastern Cape

Aliwal North 051 634 1887
Barkly East 045 971 0742
East London 043 735 1356 One of South Africa's
oldest courses and one of the leading golf venues
Fish River 040 676 1002 The Old Woman's River
meanders through the Gary Player designed layout
Grahamstown 046 622 2106
Humewood 041 583 2137 Designed by Colonel
SV Hotchkins and regarded as his finest work
Port Elizabeth 041 374 3140 Over 100 years old,
and recently upgraded
Royal Port Alfred 046 624 4796 Built between
1907-15; royal status from King George V in 1924
St Francis Bay 042 294 0467
Uitenhage 041 966 1868
Walmer Country Club 041 581 4211
Wedgewood Park 041 372 1212

9-Hole Golf Courses in the Eastern Cape

Aberdeen 049 846 0290
Adelaide 046 684 0489
Alexandria 046 653 0207
Bedford 046 685 0123
Burgersdorp 051 653 1982
Butterworth 047 491 4370
Cathcart 045 843 1170
Cradock 048 881 4548
Dirk Fourie Trust 042 285 0321
Dordrecht 082 596 5822
Elliot 045 931 1211
Fort Beaufort 046 645 1959
Gonubie 043 740 5645
Graaff-Reinet 049 893 0286
Hankey 042 284 0335
Humansdorp 042 291 0529
Indiwe 082 924 8234
Jansenville 049 834 9034
Kei Mouth 043 841 1083
Kirkwood 042 230 0452
Komga 043 831 1069
Lady Grey 051 603 0006
Langkloof 042 273 2186
Maclear 045 932 1566
Middelburg 049 842 2044
Molteno 045 967 0251
Shark River 041 581 6188
Steynsburg 048 887 0019
Steytlerville 049 835 0155
Stutterheim 043 683 1508
Walmer GC 041 581 1613
Willowmore 044 923 1679
Email gouldgolf@global.co.za for more information

Trails

Alexandria Hiking Trail, Alexandria
042 233 0556
Amadiba Adventures, Wild Coast 50km
039 305 6455
Amatola Hiking Trail 043 642 2571 / 4148
(Starts from King William's Town and ends
near Hogsback village)
Dolphin Trail, Tsitsikamma 17km
042 281 1607, 281 1836
Ecowa Trail, Elliot 47km 045 931 1011
(Municipality)
Kariega Game Reserve Trail 8-10km
043 636 7904 / 0263
Katberg Loop Trail, Balfour 18km
043 642 1747
Lammergeier, Lady Grey 051 603 1114
Mkambati Nature Reserve, Flagstaff
039 306 9000 / 727 3273
Otter Trail, Tsitsikamma 42km 042 281 1607
Settlers Hiking Trail, Port Alfred 046 625 0660
Sunshine Coast Trails, Port Alfred
046 624 5295
Strandloper Hiking Trail, Kei Mouth
043 841 1046, strandloper@net4u.co.za
strandlopertrail.tripod.com
The Lily Pad Hiking Trail, Port Alfred 12km
046 625 0815
Transkaroo Hiking Trail, Middelburg
049 843 1506, 082 441 5605
transkaroo@adsactive.com
Wild Coast Meander 55km
Wild Coast Amble 56km
Wild Coast Pondo Walk 46km
043 743 6181
Wild Coast Trails 039 305 6455
bookings@wild-coast.co.za
www.wild-coast.co.za
Woodcliffe Cave, Maclear 39km
011 412 1888, 082 653 3197

Shorter Trails & Others

Addo National Park Trail 042 233 0556
Addo National Park, Zuurberg Trail
Baviaanskloof Hiking Trails 040 635 2115
Bloukrans Walking Tours 042 281 1458
Cape St Francis Nature Reserve 042 394 0420
Cradock Bushman Trail, Mountain Zebra Trail
048 881 2427 / 2383
Graaff-Reinet Karoo Trail 049 892 3453
Grahamstown Area, Valley of the Ancient Voices
4 hour Guided Walking Trail
046 622 3241 / 8511

Groendal Hiking Trail 041 992 5418
Humansdorp Boskloof Nature Reserve
042 295 1361
Hogsback Walking Trails, Amatola Guesthouse
045 962 1059
Hogsback Trails 082 603 5246
Nieu-Bethesda, Ganora Guest Farm, Guided
Fossil Walks 049 841 1302, 841 1659
Nukakamma Canoe Trail, Sundays River Mouth
041 468 0238
Port Elizabeth, Gamtoos River Mouth
041 585 8884
Sundays River Valley Hiking Trails & Horse
Riding, Addo Elephant National Park
042 233 0556
Tsitsikamma Big Tree & Ratel, Blue Duiker
Trail, Loerie Trail, Storms River Trail
042 281 1607

Private Game Reserves, National Parks & Nature Reserves

Addo Elephant National Park 042 233 0556
reservations@parks-sa.co.za
www.parks-sa.co.za/addo
www.addoelephantpark.co.za
Amakhala Game Reserve 042 235 1608
centralres@telkomsa.net, www.amakhala.co.za
Baviaanskloof Nature Reserve 040 635 2115
info@ectourism.co.za, www.ectourism.co.za
www.baviaans.co.za
Burchell Game Reserve 042 231 1302
www.burchellgamereserve.com
Commando Drift, Tarkastad, Friendly N6
048 881 3925, 040 635 2115 (reservations)
bird@eci.co.za
Double Drift Game Reserve, Frontier Country
040 653 8010, 635 2115 (reservations)
Dwesa / Cwebe Reserves, Wild Coast
040 635 2115
Hluleka Nature Reserve, Wild Coast
040 635 2115
Inkwenkwezi Private Game Reserve, Cintsa
Wild Coast 043 734 3234
pgr@inkwenkwezi.co.za, www.inkwenkwezi.com
Kamala Game Reserve 042 243 3507
Kariega Game Reserve, Kenton-on-Sea
046 636 7904 reservations@kariega.co.za
www.kariega.co.za
Kwandwe Private Game Reserve, Grahamstown
046 603 3400, 011 809 4300 (reservations)
reception@kwandwe.co.za, www.ccafrica.com
Kwantu Private Game Reserve, Greater Addo-
Paterson 084 500 0345, 083 500 0344
info@kwantu.co.za, www.kwantu.co.za

Resources Resources Resources

Lalibela Game Reserve, Addo 041 581 8170
inquiry@lalibela.co.za, www.lalibela.co.za
Lombardini Game Reserve, Jeffreys Bay
042 293 2073, 082 655 4370
www.lombardinifarm.com
Mkambati Nature Reserve, Wild Coast
040 635 2115
Misty Mountain Reserve, Tsitsikamma
042 280 3699 www.misty-sa.co.za
mistymountainsreserve@intekom.co.za
Molweni Private Game Reserve, Grahamstown
046 684 0261 www.koedoeskloof.co.za
Mountain Zebra National Park, Cradock, Karoo
Heartland 048 881 2427, 012 428 9111
www.parks-sa.co.za
Mpofu Game Reserve, Fort Beaufort
040 635 2115
Mpongo Private Game Reserve 043 709 5038
info@premierhotels.co.za
Nyala Valley Game Park, Port Elizabeth
046 625 0815, 082 375 9567
www.nyalavalley.co.za
Schotia Safaris Private Game Reserve
042 235 1436
Seaview Game and Lion Park, Port Elizabeth
041 378 1702 seaview@isat.co.za
www.seaviewgamepark.co.za
Shamwari Private Game Reserve
042 203 1111 shamwaribookings@global.co.za
www.shamwari.com
Silaka Reserve Wild Coast 040 635 2115
Timbila Game Reserve
044 923 1816, 084 616 6845
info@timbila-bhejane.com, www.timbila-
bhejane.co.za www.timbila.co.za
Tsitsikamma National Park
042 281 1607, 280 3561 www.tsistikamma.net
adventure@gardenroute.co.za
Tsolwana Game Reserve, between Queenstown
and Tarkastad 040 845 1112, 635 2115
Umgamanzi Game Lodge & Safaris
041 961 0359

Nature Conservation Eastern Cape
040 635 2115, 043 701 9600
reservations@ectourism.co.za
Info@ectourism.co.za, www.ectourism.co.za
Aliwal North 051 633 3569
East London 043 701 9600
King William's Town 043 642 2571
Wild Coast Region: Coffee Bay 047 531 1191
(info@ectourism.co.za), Umtata 047 532 2445

South African National Parks Board
012 428 9111, 343 0905
www.parks-sa.co.za
reservations@parks-sa.co.za

ACCOMMODATION
Addo
Darlington Lake Lodge 042 243 3673
Gorah Elephant Camp 044 532 7818
River Bend Country Lodge 042 233 0160

Alexandria Bushmans River Mouth
Heritage Lodge Guest House 046 653 0024
Kikuyu Lodge 046 653 9039
Sandon On Sea 046 654 0217

Amatola Mountains Escape
Mpofu Nature Reserve
040 635 2115, 864 9450

Beacon Bay
Blue Lagoon Hotel 043 748 4821
blhotel@iafrica.com, www.bluelagoonhotel.co.za

Bathurst
Protea Hotel Bathurst 046 625 0833
Pig & Whistle Hotel 046 625 0673
abmtrade@global.co.za, www.pigandwhistle.co.za

Bedford
Cavers Country House 046 685 0619
ckross@intekom.co.za, www.cavers.co.za

Cintsa / Wild Coast
Broomstick 043 734 3269
Cintsa Lodge 043 738 5146
Crawfords Cabins 043 738 5000
Inkwenkwezi Private Game Reserve
043 734 3234

Cradock
Die Tuishuis 048 881 1322
tuishuise@eastcape.net, www.tuishuise.co.za
Heritage House 048 881 3210
Mountain Zebra Park 012 428 9111
Oude Pastorie Lodge 048 881 3011
Pam House 048 881 4229
Southern Cross Safaris 048 886 0606

East London
Blue Lagoon Hotel 043 748 4821
Chelsea Square 043 743 0397

Clevedon B&B 043 722 7423
Devereux Lodge 043 726 9459
Dolphin View Lodge 043 702 8600
King David Protea Hotel 043 722 3174
Lagoon Valley Resort 043 736 97 53
Meander Inn 043 726 2310
Quarry Lake Inn 043 707 5400
Quintetta Guest Farm 043 748 4729

Elliot
Merino Hotel 045 931 2987
Mountain Shadows Hotel 045 931 2233
Myburgh Lodge 045 931 1546
Rose Garden 045 931 1158, 082 771 8947
Tulloch 043 740 0470, 082 932 8086
Woodpeckers Lodge 045 931 1402

Friendly N6
Tsolwana Nature Reserve 040 635 2115

Frontier Country
Double Drift 040 635 2115
Kwandwe Game Reserve 011 809 4300
Molweni Private Game Reserve 046 684 0261

Gonubie
Boardwalk Beach House 043 740 2290
Germany Bay Lodge 083 625 1181
Gonubie Point Guest House
043 740 4279, 082 824 1419
Seaspray 043 740 4234
The Crowned Crane 082 568 2274
The Gonubie Sun B&B 043 740 4507
The White House B&B 043 740 0344

Graaff-Reinet
Avondrust Guest House 049 892 3566
Die Pophuise 049 891 0404
Drostdy Hotel 049 892 2161
drostdy@intekom.co.za
Eenzaamheid Holiday Farm 049 845 9011
Langfontein Guest Farm
049 845 9021, 082 655 6900

Grahamstown
Lantern Hill B&B 046 622 8782
Oak Lodge Hotel 046 622 9123
Protea Hotel Evelyn House 046 622 2366
Protea Hotel Grahamstown 046 622 2324
Settlers Hill Cottages 046 622 9720
The Cock House 046 636 1287 / 95
082 820 5592 www.cockhouse.co.za

Albany Hotel Group 046 622 2366
www.albanyhotels.co.za

Greater Addo Paterson
Amakhala 042 235 1608
Dreamers Armadale B&B 042 230 0908
Highfields B&B 042 235 1269
Lalibela Game Reserve 041 581 8170
Sandflats B&B and Self-Catering 042 235 1012
Shamwari 042 203 1111

Hankey
Schumba Safari Lodge 042 284 0828

Hogsback
Granny Mouse House 045 962 1259
Hyde Park Chalets 045 962 1069
Kings Lodge 045 962 1024
Lowestoff Country Lodge 045 843 1716
The Edge 045 962 1159

Jeffreys Bay
Al Kynaston 042 296 1845
Beach Music 042 2932291
Beaufort 7 042 296 2092
Costa Cara 042 293 4160
Diaz 15 042 293 1779
Dirkie's Dream 042 293 3909
Eastview B&B 042 296 1484
Greystone Guest House 042 296 0616
Lazee Bay B&B 042 296 2090
Opp-I-See B&B 042 296 1355
Sandkasteel 042 293 1585
Savoy Hotel 042 293 1106
Stratos Guest House 042 293 1116
Supertubes Guest House 042 293 2957
The Haven 042 296 1926
The White House 042 293 3116

Kenton-On-Sea
Amblewood 046 648 2957
Burke's Nest 046 648 1894
Carriage House 046 648 1129
Hillcrest House B&B 046 648 2961
Kariega Game Reserve 046 636 7904
Lime Tree House 046 648 1226
The Milking Parlour 046 622 8395
Wings 046 648 1834
Woodlands Country Cottages
046 648 2867
Woodside B&B 046 648 1802

King William's Town
Dreamers Guest House 043 642 3012

Langkloof
Louterwater Landgoed 042 272 1724
The Kraaltjie Guest House 082 498 1045

Middelburg
Bundu Safaris Karoo 049 842 2910
Carlton Heights 049 842 2017
Hillston Farm 049 842 1627
Karoo Country Inn 049 842 1126
Mount Melsetter Karoo 049 842 1520

Patensie
Baviaanskloof Nature Reserve 040 635 2115
Craggy Burn 042 284 0673
Droëkloof Buschcamp
042 284 0729, 082 874 4714
Gonjah Chalet 042 283 0596
Orchard View Guest House
042 283 0248, 084 240 7057
Waterwiel B&B 042 283 0491

Port Alfred
Fish River Sun 040 676 1101
Medolino Resort 046 624 1651
Nyala Valley Game Park 046 625 0815
Oribi Haven 046 648 2043, 084 477 1166
The Halyards Hotel 046 624 2410
The Residency 046 624 5382
Villa Majestic 046 624 2857

Port Elizabeth
Africa Beach B&B 041 583 5833
Apron Strings 041 366 2320 / 1217
Beacon Lodge 041 583 5061
Beach Hotel 041 583 2161
Brookes Hill Suites 041 586 0990
Bishops Lodge 041 585 6828
Edward Protea Hotel 041 586 2056
Humewood Hotel 041 585 8961
Ikhayalam Lodge 041 582 5098
Kasama Lodge 041 583 4579
King's Tide Boutique Hotel 041 583 6023
Margate Place Guest House 041 583 5799
Park Place 041 585 5062
Paxton Hotel 041 585 9655
Summerstrand Inn 041 583 3131
Summer House B&B 041 583 4854
Sylvesters Guest House 041 373 1889
The Kelwey Hotel 041 584 0638

Victorian Villa Guest Manor 041 373 5359
Villa Hestia 041 503 8500
Wilma's Guest House 041 583 1527

Rhodes
Rhodes Hotel 045 974 9305
Tiffendell Ski Resort 011 787 9090

Somerset East
Noah's Art 042 243 1925
Somerset House 042 243 1819 / 3935
Witmos Oxwagon Camp 048 886 0630
De Opstal B&B 042 243 2566 ,082 831 0713

St Francis Bay
Cape St Francis Resort 042 298 0054
Lyngenfjord House 042 298 0444
Milkwood Country Cottages 042 294 1007
Port St Francis 042 294 1223
Samaki 042 294 0270
Sandriver Lodge 042 294 1052
Two Moons 042 294 1647
Waterways B&B 042 294 0282

Stutterheim
The Manderson 043 683 2322

Sundays River Valley / Addo
Addo Elephant National Park 042 233 0556
Chrislin B&B 042 233 0022
Cosmos Cuisine 042 234 0323
Good Hope Country House 042 234 0357
Gorah Elephant Camp 044 532 7818
Homestead B&B 042 233 0354
Riverbend Country Lodge 042 233 0161
Stellenhof Country House 042 233 2423
Valleyview B&B 042 233 0349
Zuurberg Mountain Inn 042 233 0583

Tarkastad
Carrickmoor Guest Farm 045 846 9252
Lesley's B&B 045 846 0481

Tsitsikamma
Misty Mountain Reserve 042 280 3699
The Fennery 042 280 3588
Tsitsikamma Lodge 042 280 3802
info@tsitsikamma.com, www.tsitsikamma.com
Tsitsikamma National Park 042 281 1607
www.parks-sa.co.za
Tsitsikamma On Sea 042 280 3697

Wild Coast
Coffee Shack 047 575 2048
Country Lodge 047 532 5730
Cremorne Estate 047 564 1110
Haga Haga Resort 043 841 1670
Hlululeka Nature Reserve 040 635 2115
Kei Mouth Beach Hotel 043 841 1017
Kob Inn 047 499 0011
Lily Lodge 047 564 1229
Mbotyi River Lodge 039 253 8822
mbotyi@pondoland.co.za, www.mbotyi.co.za
Mitford Lodge 043 841 1510
Mkabati Nature Reserve 040 635 2115
Morgan Bay Hotel 043 841 1062
Ocean View Hotel 047 575 2005
oceanview@coffeebay.co.za
Seagulls Beach Hotel 047 498 0044
rod@seagulls.co.za, www.seagulls.co.za
Silaka Nature Reserve 040 635 2115
The Estuary Country Hotel Port Edward
039 311 2675, www.estuary.co.za
Trennery's Hotel 047 498 0004
Umngazi River Bungalows 047 564 1115/6/7
Umngazi@iafrica.com, www.umngazi.co.za
Wavecrest Resort Hotel 047 498 0022
Wild Coast Sun 011 780 7800

Willowmore
Timbila Game Reserve 084 616 6845

CARAVAN AND CAMPING
Alexandria Beyond Adventure Campsite
046 654 0219, 043 743 5778

Addo Addo Elephant National Park
042 233 0556 / 0196

Aliwal North Aliwal Spa 051 633 2951

Bushmans River Mouth Boesmans Caravan
Park 046 648 3584

Cannon Rocks Cannon Rocks Holiday Resort
046 654 0043 / 0095

Cape St Francis Holiday Resort 042 298 0054

Cintsa East Cintsa Bay Holiday Resort &
Caravan Park 043 738 5064 / 5544
Arendsnes 043 734 3015

Cradock Commando Drift Nature Reserve &
Dam 048 881 3925

East London Glen Eden Resort 043 734 3033
Club Arena Riverside Resort 043 734 3055
Lagoon Valley 043 736 9753 / 9796
Palm Springs 043 781 1901 / 1990

Gonubie Gonubie Caravan Park
043 705 9750, 740 5937

Graaff-Reinet Urquart Caravan Park
049 892 2136, 891 0427

Grahamstown Grahamstown Caravan Park
046 622 9112, 622 3241

Hamburg Hamburg Caravan Park
040 678 0042

Jeffreys Bay Jeffreys Bay Caravan Park and
Campsite 042 293 1111 ext 241

Port Alfred
Medolino Caravan Park 046 624 1651 / 2514
Riverside Caravan Park 046 624 2230 / 2702
Willows Caravan Park 046 624 5201 / 3666

Port Elizabeth
Pine Lodge HR 041 583 4004 / 3839
Humepark Recreation Club 041 585 4013
Willows Holiday Resort 041 366 1717 / 1878
Van Stadens River Mouth 041 776 1059 / 1077

Somerset East Besterhoek Caravan Park
042 243 1333 / 1548

Stutterheim Kologha Camping Site
043 683 2474

Tsitsikamma Storms River Mouth
042 281 1607, 012 428 9111
Khoisan Caravan Park 042 281 1450 / 1457

Wild Coast Central Reservations 047 531 1191
Cremorne Estate 047 564 1113
Morgan Bay Caravan Park 043 841 1062
Kei Mouth Caravan & Camping 043 841 1004
Wild Coast Holidays 043 743 6181
www.wildcoastholidays.co.za
Fish River Sun Hotel and Country Club Resort
040 676 1101 fishsun@sunint.co.za
www.suninternational.com